I Love Being
a Mom

———❧———

I Love Being a Mom

a Mom

Treasured Stories,
Memories, and Milestones

Edited by

Therese J. Borchard

Doubleday

New York   Toronto   London   Auckland   Sydney

PUBLISHED BY DOUBLEDAY
a division of Random House, Inc.
1745 Broadway, New York, New York 10019

DOUBLEDAY and the portrayal of an anchor with a dolphin are trademarks
of Doubleday, a division of Random House, Inc.

Pages 228–235 consist of an extension of this copyright page.

Library of Congress Cataloging-in-Publication Data
I love being a mom : treasured stories, memories, and milestones / edited by
Therese J. Borchard.—1st ed.
p. cm.
1. Mothers—Anecdotes. 2. Mother and child—Anecdotes.
3. Motherhood—Anecdotes. 4. Motherhood in popular culture.
5. Mothers—Quotations, maxims, etc. 6. Motherhood—Quotations,
maxims, etc. I. Borchard, Therese Johnson.
HQ759.I44 2004
306.874'3—dc21
2003055410

0-385-50789-5

PRINTED IN THE UNITED STATES OF AMERICA

March 2004

First Edition

1 3 5 7 9 10 8 6 4 2

For David and newborn Katherine Rose

the reasons why I love being a mom

One thing about having a baby is that each step of the way

you simply cannot imagine loving him any more than

you already do, because you are bursting with love,

loving as much as you are humanly capable of—and

then you do, you love him even more.

ANNE LAMOTT

CONTENTS

I Love Being a Mom

What do Anna Quindlen, Debbie Reynolds, and Katie Couric have in common with more than a billion women around the globe from Sydney to San Diego? They've screamed in labor, carried a diaper bag, and held on their chest the most precious bundle of joy ever known to them. They are mothers, they love it, and they say why in this book.

I Love Being a Mom celebrates the treasured traditions, rituals, and stories that run through the bloodstream of mothers everywhere. "Biology is the least of what makes someone a mother," says Oprah Winfrey. It is the memories and experiences that form the real umbilical cord, the tears and laughter that connect mothers to their children more intimately than the placenta inside the womb.

"Then someone placed her in my arms. She looked up at me. . . . Her eyes melted through me, forging a connection in me with their soft heat," Shirley Maclaine writes. "He was the most beautiful thing I had even seen. He was moonlight," describes Anne Lamott.

This book is about the favorite snapshots of motherhood women have compiled over time: The first audible heartbeat. An eighteen-week sonogram. A first tooth. The first day of school. Shopping for a prom dress. A call home from college. It's about the common bond that all mothers share, and the unique experiences of each. It's about the little hand that every mother holds and the individual fingerprint of each child; the milestones discussed at playgroup and the sacred moments reserved for two.

It's about why a foster mom and a stepmom know the same raw joy and distress as a mom who shares her kid's genes. And why all three would agree that the love they feel for their children is unimaginable.

From conception to adulthood, the essays and quotes in *I Love Being a Mom* remind women of how radically their lives change when they become mothers, stretching their hearts with their bellies and initiating them into a special club whose responsibilities go way beyond changing diapers and playing house. The book also spotlights memorable movies, novels, songs, and TV sitcoms that peek at mothers of all generations.

This family album of a book is about what the philosopher Pierre Teilhard de Chardin called "the chosen part of things." It endeavors to show, in word and picture, with love and joy, why so many women forget about the labor pains of delivery and proclaim long after the nursery drapes have gone out of style, "I love being a mom!"

—Therese J. Borchard

Crossing Over

By Naomi Wolf

We were a new family with one small magnetic creature and two sleep-deprived adults, drawn to the little one's needs as if under an enchantment. I could not remember when we had last seen a movie, or worn unstained clothing, or slept through the night. I could scarcely recall the self I had been before. The life of our new family had begun to knit. For almost four weeks, the baby had been an eldritch presence in our home: we would wash and feed and dote on her. Still, we had to take her babyhood on faith, for she was still a half-alien, half-animal being, waving her little limbs, turning her smooth, warm little head suddenly, inexplicably, as if listening to bulletins, inaudible to anyone else, from her home planet.

One night, though—one night: The baby and I were alone. I was sitting on the green couch with her; the couch where I had slowly fallen in love with something I did not fathom, something I was imperceptibly part of.

One night I crossed over.

Branches and leaves pressed around the windows of our

apartment. Wind chimes were suspended in the branches outside. The chimes shivered a little. A silver tremor of sound hung in the air.

The little one took her mouth from my nipple, and her head turned toward the sound. She held perfectly still until the notes subsided. She was listening to music.

She was a human baby, listening.

Her mother held her.

"Do you hear the bells, Rosie?" I whispered. "Can you hear the bells?"

Naomi Wolf is the bestselling author of *The Beauty Myth* and *Misconceptions*. She lives in New York City.

ONE

The Making of a Mother

A mother's love doesn't begin with the mother, or the child, let alone a set of rules or recommendations or anything having to do with the mind. A mother's love comes on like a thunderstorm. You may or may not hear the low rumble as it approaches, you may or may not have time to close your windows and call in your cat. But when the storm comes the storm is all there is. The sky opens and weeps and howls and devours.

—Jeanne Marie Laskas
Washington, D.C.

Giving birth is little more than a set of muscular contractions granting passage of a child. Then the mother is born.

—Erma Bombeck

Making the decision to have a child—it's momentous. It is to decide forever to have your heart go walking around outside your body.

—Elizabeth Stone

The Lightning Bugs Are Back

By Anna Quindlen

The lightning bugs are back. They are small right now, babies really, flying low to the ground as the lawn dissolves from green to black in the dusk. There are constellations of them outside the window: on, off, on, off. At first the little boy cannot see them; then, suddenly, he does. "Mommy, it's magic," he says.

This is why I had children: because of the lightning bugs. Several years ago I was reading a survey in a women's magazine and I tried to answer the questions: Did you decide to have children: A. because of family pressure; B. because it just seemed like the thing to do; C. because of a general liking for children; D. because of religious mandates; E. none of the above.

I looked for the lightning bugs; for the answer that said because sometime in my life I wanted to stand at a window with a child and show him the lightning bugs and have him say, "Mommy, it's magic." And since nothing even resembling that answer was there, I assumed that, as usual, I was a little twisted, that no one else was so reductive, so obsessed with the telling detail, had a reason so seemingly trivial for a decision so enormous. And then the other night, yellow bug stars flickering around us, my husband said, in a rare moment of perfect unanimity: "That's it. That's why I wanted them, too."

The lightning bugs are my madeleine, my cue for a wave of selective recollection. My God, the sensation the other night when the first lightning bug turned his tail on too soon, competing with daylight during the magic hour between dusk and dark. I felt like the anthropologist I once met, who could take a little chunk of femur or a knucklebone and from it describe age, sex, perhaps even height and weight.

From this tiny piece of bone I can reconstruct a childhood: a hot night under tall trees. Squares of lighted windows up and down the dark street. A wiffle ball game in the middle of the road, with the girls and the littlest boys playing the outfield. The Good-Humor man, in his solid, square truck, the freezer smoky and white when he reaches inside for a Popsicle or a Dixie cup. The dads sitting inside in their Bermuda shorts watching *Car 54, Where are You?* The moms in the kitchen finishing the dishes. The dull hum of the fans in the bedroom windows. The cheap crack of the wiffle bat. The bells of the ice-cream truck. The lightning bugs trapped in empty peanut-butter jars that have triangular holes in the lids, made with the point of a beer-can opener. The fading smears of phosphorescent yellow-green, where the older, more jaded kids have used their sneaker soles to smear the lights across the gray pavement. "Let them out," our mothers say, "or they will die in there." Finally, perfect sleep. Sweaty sheets. No dreams.

We were careless. We always forgot to open the jars. The lightning bugs would be there in the morning, their yellow tails dim in the white light of the summer sun, their feet pathetic as they lay on their backs, dead as anything. We were always surprised and a bit horrified by what we had done, or had failed to do. As night fell we shook them out and caught more.

This is why I had children: to offer them a perfect dream of childhood that can fill their souls as they grow older, even as they know that it is only one bone from a sometimes troubled body. And to fill my own soul, too, so that I can relive the magic of the yellow light without the bright white of hindsight, to see only the glow and not the dark. Mommy, it's magic, those little flares in the darkness, a distillation of the kind of life we think we had, we wish we had, we want again.

Anna Quindlen is a nationally syndicated columnist, novelist, and mother living in New Jersey.

❧

It's like you grow another heart, like someone kicks down a door that was sealed shut, and then the whole world—sunshine, flowers—falls through. I have such joy that I didn't think was possible.

—Rosie O'Donnell

Even though I'm not a terribly religious person, I feel that this child was born for me.

—Barbara Walters

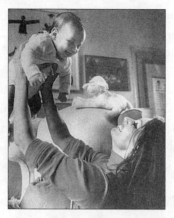

Actress Sophia Loren and her
newborn son, Carlo Ponti, Jr., in
1969. © Alfred Eisenstaedt, Timepix

When you are a mother, you are never really alone in your thoughts. You are connected to your child and to all those who touch your lives. A mother always has to think twice, once for herself and once for her child.

—Sophia Loren

What It Means to Be a Mother

By Katrina Kenison

When I was pregnant with my first child, I spent hours visualizing various delivery scenes, trying in vain to imagine how it would feel to give birth. I worried about birth defects and premature labor, practiced breathing, experimented with recommended delivery positions, and, like a good student, I read practical guidebooks about breast-feeding and newborn care. I thought I was preparing, as well as I could, to have a baby. But my daydreams rarely took me beyond the delivery room; birth itself was the main event, the one that seemed at once so frightening and so exciting. Once the baby arrived, well, it went without saying—we would all come home and begin our life together as a family.

How could I have spent so much time thinking about the birth process and so little envisioning what might lie beyond it? Perhaps, deep down, I realize that there was no preparing for the experience of motherhood itself, or for the irrevocable transformation that would occur as my son was delivered out of my body and into my arms. A new person took his place on earth in that moment, and, in the same instant, I became new. I was a mother. From that moment on, I have seen the world through different eyes.

As mothers, we are bound by depths of pain and waves of joy that those who have not raised children will never know. In each of our children we see a miracle of life—even as we realize, with sudden insight, that the world is full of just such miracles. I called my own mother at three A.M.—as the obstetrician sat on a stool between my legs, stitching my episiotomy with long black thread—and told her she was a grandmother. An hour and a half later, she slipped into my room, having driven alone in the dark, without direction, to a city hospital she had never been to before. She talked her way past the security guards and the night nurses, and she came to me. I was not altogether surprised to see her, though; it was just beginning to dawn on me what it means to be a mother.

Katrina Kenison is the author of *Mitten Strings for God* and the mother of two sons.

⇜

When a child enters the world through you, it alters everything on a psychic, psychological, and purely practical level.
—Jane Fonda

Actress Jane Fonda at home with her daughter. © Bill Ray/Timepix

I was changed forever. From a woman whose "womb" had been, in a sense, her head—that is to say, certain small seeds had gone in, and rather different if not larger or better "creations" had come out—to a woman who . . . had two wombs!
                                        —Alice Walker

When my daughter was born something inside me which had long been slumbering kicked into gear. It has been functioning, neurotically and unbidden, ever since.
                                        —Barbara Zucker
                                        New York, New York

The baby is born and your life is changed more than you ever dreamed. You find you have sprouted invisible antennae that pick up every alteration in breathing, every variation in temperature, every nuance of expression in your tiny daughter. No one tells you that the change is irreversible. That you will feel in your heart every pain, every loss, every disappointment, every rebuff, every cruelty that she experiences life long.

                                        —Pam Brown

I didn't want to be pregnant. Or so I thought, through my vehement twenties and well into my still-strident thirties. I was a seventies' feminist for whom a woman's creative freedom meant a room of one's own and no one to answer to whenever I felt like taking in a late-night poetry reading or catching a train to some political event. I could not stop for the minutiae of motherhood, I told myself, when the world itself was like a sick child—hungry, homeless, crazed with material dreams—and in desperate need of advocacy. Mother love? No Pampers or strained peaches for me. Rather, I would channel my nurtur-

ing energies into social causes, a writer with a sort of feminized earth-mother soul.

But the more I wrote, the less I believed in the power of words alone to heal. I came to see that just as all politics in the end are personal, so too is life's deepest poetry. Meaning began at home, and all the pain in the world wasn't deep enough to wipe out the impulse for personal renewal.

Thus, on the cusp of forty, I began trying to conceive a child. For five years I existed in a shadow land of yearning and disappointment. I learned what it was to want what I could not will. As I sat in clinic offices staring at photographs of alpine meadows and gorgeous mountain vistas intended to help me think positive thoughts, I grew more deeply engulfed in a grief that even loved ones could not know existed. The stories of mothers and their children were like enchantments to me, meditations from a state that I began to believe I would never attain.

And then one miraculous October day, a heart beat alongside mine. Hands reached toward the light through the amniotic ocean. The first time I saw my son's two-chambered heart, I wept. And the moment, eight and a half months later, when I heard his first yelp of assertion upon arriving in the world, I knew that creation had begun anew. As his ruddy head rooted at my breast, rapt with the newness of sense and hunger, I realized that to love this child through the arduous struggle into manhood would be the greatest creative act I would ever perform.

—Kathleen Hirsch
Boston, Massachusetts

There's a grating suppression in the pit of my stomach. It's a resisting, guttural reaction to the fact that my life is inescapably constructed around motherhood. Biologically and psychologi-

Bernadette Price with son Tommy.

cally, as a social construction and as a familial one, I am defined as a mother and always will be.

—Janet Maloney Franze
Richmond, Virginia

As a first-timer at age forty-three, my outlook on life after the first twelve weeks of motherhood combined apprehension with exhaustion. What did I know about taking care of a baby? Even with a supportive husband and a nearly live-in grandma, I found it hard to reconcile the awesome responsibility with my apparent (to me) inadequacy. I felt as helpless as, well, a baby!

One late-night feeding, as Tommy drifted to sleep, I got up from the rocking chair to lay him back down in his crib. Cuddled up to my chest, he very gently laid one tiny baby hand directly over my heart. In the warmth and weight of his touch, terror and exhaustion gave way to an indescribable feeling of peace and wonder and gratitude.

And then my little angel pursed his tiny lips and blew his first perfect baby raspberry.

As I shook with silent laughter trying not to wake him, I knew I was truly a mommy. I still feel sometimes overwhelmed—that goes with the territory—but it's really joy disguised as something else. It's mommyhood.

—Bernadette Price
Mahopac, New York

You will love your baby with such a fierce single-mindedness that being someone's mother is the only endeavor on earth that you will be certain nature fully intended for you.

—Vicki Iovine

Interlude ❧

Celine Dion holds her newly
baptized son, Rene-Charles.
© Jim Young/Reuters/Timepix

It's like life holds a secret, and having a child is that
secret.

—Celine Dion

I knew that I would love my child, but I had no idea it
would fill me with such a sense of completion.

—Rosie O'Donnell

It has been the greatest wonder of my life to know the love of my own child and to see the way a child develops a loving heart for people.

—Kathie Lee Gifford

I've seen my name in letters as tall as a house. I've been toasted by audiences who've seen me on international television. I've won virtually every major award my career offers. I say all of that simply to say this: I've never been as fulfilled as I was when my son was born.

—Reba McEntire

I've always been amazed by the miracle of it all. And the mystery.

—Christie Brinkley

TWO

It's Good to Be a Mom

My daughter made me ecstatic; my love for her eclipsed any other. She gave me back the parks and the circus and bright colors. She bestowed upon me a set of friends I could never have found on my own, made me a lot less judgmental, a much nicer person, got me to Disney World, put me back in touch with my parents, and fundamentally connected me to the universe.

—Barbara Zucker
New York, New York

On a macrolevel, I like knowing that I've had a role in bringing two compassionate, smart people into the world, who have the potential to make it better. On a personal level, I like the fact that the kids have forced me to develop different sides of myself than I would have without their presence in my life.

—Wendy Schuman
Montclair, New Jersey

My favorite aspect of motherhood is the sheer hilarity of it. Our three-year-old has a sublime sense of the ridiculous, and we never know what will come out of her mouth next. Of course, the most hysterical things she says are the ones she doesn't necessarily intend to be funny—such as when I was tucking her into bed the other night. She was reluctant to fall asleep, so I reassured her that tomorrow would be another fun day, full of playing. She seemed pleased about that and started enumerating

Jana Riess and daughter Jerusha.

how her morning would begin. "I wake up, I see sun, I pick my nose!" she said excitedly. I could hardly stop laughing.

—Jana Riess
Winchester, Kentucky

Ten Good Reasons to Be a Mom

By Sharon Lebell

1. Being a mom is an express ticket to a meaningful life.

You've no doubt met your share of people who are perpetually in a fret about the meaning of their lives. Most likely, they aren't moms. While moms are just as self-reflective and self-aware as anyone else, trying to find their existential call-

Sharon Lebell with her children.

ing, overcoming anomie, or other vaguely Sartre-esqe indulgences are just not mom-things-to-do. Moms don't need to bother with all that Sturm and Drang.

Since we're mercifully not mired in doubts about our significance, we have a clear-sighted view of what actually makes life meaningful. We are free to experience a largesse of personal meaning every day, because we are busy making it ourselves in our relationships with our children. And when we are not busy being mom-meaning-makers (in our roles of creators and transmitters of tradition, values, and culture, or, perhaps more mundanely, sewing Halloween costumes), we are meaning appreciators and discoverers. There's no avoiding this.

2. *Moms have compassion . . . for everybody.*
Moms are endowed with compassion. This isn't because we were born with halos. It is because we moms traffic in mistakes. Kids make them all the time, and we moms make them and regret them and anguish over having made them all the time. Being around kids is an exercise in entropy tolerance, in plans upended—flexibility required, or you'll drive yourself nuts.

Kids are indeed amazing people, but heaven knows they also spill their cereal, forget their homework, and when they are teenagers, sometimes give you such a withering evil eye, you wonder whether your teen is the same person you nursed and unremittingly adored thirteen plus years ago.

Moms have two choices: We can be continually tense, exasperated, and disillusioned with our imperfect children and our imperfect selves, or we can get smart and notice that imperfection and goofs are just endemic to humans.

Even occasional unbidden evil eyes are part of the human package. (Put this in your "Oh Well" file.) Most of the time, moms choose option two, acceptance of the human animal with all of its foibles. This acceptance naturally expresses itself as compassion for others: starting with our own kids, extending to ourselves, thence to a kinder retrospective understanding of our own parents' blunders and shortfalls, and finally, if we're lucky, to humanity in general.

3.   Want to build your character? Be a mom!

Kids keep you honest and true to your ideals. Pick your virtue! Do you want to be more patient, a better listener? How about some inner strength, discipline, steadiness? Then be a mom, because then you'll be in the virtue business. This doesn't mean we are always virtuous or better than everyone else, but as forced exemplars for our kids, we have to clean up our act or take a lot of flak. There's so much explaining to do when your deeds don't square up with your words. And kids will call you on these dissonances regular as rain. Believe me, it's much easier to find and express your better self than face the inevitable kid tribunal if you've been lazy, inconsistent, or a dope.

4.   Location Location Location: Moms get to live in the United States of Reality.

Reality has its pluses and minuses, but on balance, it's the best place to live. Yes, it's full of wars and famines and countless injustices and gratuitous griefs that will break your heart over and over. It's also filled with an inordinate amount of hassle. But hold on . . . it's also filled with jaw-dropping beauty, sublime and unexpected joys, and the greatest things imaginable that can be felt and appreciated only if you're willing to expose yourself to that rawness contained in this moment, and the next, and the next. . . .

Kids will hijack your plane if you decide to take a trip elsewhere, and while you might be temporarily annoyed, you'll thank them for returning you to the best place in the world: real life.

5. *Being a mom is not what you thought it would be . . .*
. . . and kids aren't what you thought either.

After recovering from initial pique, I always chuckle to myself when some self-appointed expert, say a close relative or a friend, even someone who works with children every day, gives unsolicited parental advice. Because they don't have a clue!

Before I had children I thought I knew a lot of things. I thought I knew about love. I thought I knew about what really matters. I thought I knew how to treat people, and a thousand other smug bits of false knowledge. Negative.

Now I know, not unlike Socrates, that I grasp no certainties about anything. I learn this every day from my four kids. They are different every day as individuals. And we are different every day as a family.

Every day contains some completely unexpected kid event. Random example: two months ago my fourteen-year-old daughter announced that she was becoming a vegan and wanted to be an electric bass player. She'd never played a bass in her life. Huh? Where did this come from? It's not even worth asking. A couple of weeks ago, my husband, John, and our whole family got to proudly watch

Misha perform in her rock band, "The Fairweather Friends," and she was amazingly good!

6.   *Kids are extraordinary.*

Before I had kids of my own, I thought you had to like kids as a category in order to be a good mom. I never did, but when my own children came along, I was utterly transformed by children. My own and everyone else's. I finally understood: Yes, of course, kids are extraordinary! And they help us see the extraordinary, be extraordinary, and reach for the extraordinary. They help us see things we wouldn't see for ourselves, and they make improbable connections we wouldn't otherwise make. In other words, they are proto-geniuses and they thereby summon the genius in us.

7.   *Moms are the best time managers around.*

If you want something done, ask a mom. Want a crash course in time management? Be a mom. Moms get things done, because we have to. People ask me all the time how I do it. I write books and articles, have four really interesting and well-adjusted kids, a couple of golden retrievers who need to be walked, and a part-time music business. What's the deal here? Moms know that you can't waste time. We hear the meter ticking and we get going. If there is something that needs to be done or we want to do, we don't hem and haw. We just do it. We don't have to take the seminars or anything. We get stuff done. Why? Because we have to.

8.   *Love. Love. Love.*

I thought I knew what love was. What an arrogant smarty-pants I was. Then I had kids. 'Nuff said.

9. *Being a mom is an opportunity to feel the full spectrum of human emotion, a chance to be fully, unabashedly alive.*

Have you ever noticed what a wet-blanket culture we live in? That corniness, sincere gushing enthusiasm, and really, really caring in all its clumsy but well-meant expressions is kind of not "cool"?

I find that the greatest respite from this cardboard, insipid, pseudodignified grown-up world is the world of kids. Yes, I'm ranting. I know. And I could probably use fewer contemptuous and emotional adjectives. But kids allow this. They allow feeling, and freedom from lock-step logic, and permission to go over the top. I think we humans need this. Passion, I believe it's called. Passion with no apologies.

10. *Moms are powerful.*

Power is often associated with high business stature or holding political office: all worthwhile and useful, yes. But the day-in and day-out influence that a mom has on a child, not as an aggressive molder of personality, but as a pervasive example-setter, is the most powerful, revolutionary act there is. Perhaps it is moms who best understand that "good" power is usually unsung and obliquely imparted. But power it is, make no mistake. We're changing the world for the good one child at a time!

Sharon Lebell is the author of the bestseller *The Art of Living* and the mother of four children. She and her husband live in rural northern California.

✒

There is no greater joy in life than that of being a mother. Along with the job description comes not only chauffeur, cook, maid, and drill sergeant, but most important, gardener of souls—fertilizer, weeder, waterer, exposer to the light, and then watcher as each seedling grows and becomes its own beautiful self.

—Linda Eyre
Salt Lake City, Utah

There is nothing more thrilling in this world, I think, than having a child that is yours, and yet is mysteriously a stranger.

—Agatha Christie

If there were no other reasons (though we know there are as many as stars), this alone would be the value of children: the way they remind you of the comfort of simplicity. Their compelling common sense. Their accessibility and their honesty. Their lack of pretense.

—Elizabeth Berg

Children are a gift to humanity. They come with open arms, wide hearts, and all the love in the world. To receive these gifts as a mother is the greatest blessing on earth.

—Nancy E. Borchard
Annapolis, Maryland

Interlude ꦿ

Great with Child
By Debra Rienstra

A marvelous mystery. A person has taken root inside me, but I do not know who this will be. I know nothing about the genetic permutations already thrown together (except whose bodies they came from), nothing about the character of soul this person might be given. When my imagination tries eagerly to fill in the mystery, I curb it.

We must not "rush into the silent spots," one of my professors used to say about the beautiful and often cryptic Old Testament narratives. I do not want to rush into this new person's silence before he or she has a chance to become.

Some women feel mysterious connections to their unborn children before they even qualify medically as fetuses. Some poets write in direct address to these cell-children: "and you, like the powerful muscle/we call heart, grow stronger within me." But I can't get that far, can't make that kind of second-person construction. My parental tasks are to nurture, to love, to understand, and to teach. Eventually.

For now my job is simply a kind of loving waiting, a surprisingly passive patience while the automatic, relentless power of life will grow this tiny mustard seed into the very obvious, present, and sheltering little sapling of someone entirely new.

There are preparations to be made. But they are mostly from the point of view of the world, not of the child.

I must make a place in my life, in my family, and in this world for a new person. Part the seas, make the rough places plain, make the crooked straight, because this person will change the terrain, as surely and persistently as tree roots burst a sidewalk apart.

Debra Rienstra is the author of *Great with Child: On Becoming a Mother.* She lives in Grand Rapids, Michigan.

THREE

Big, Bigger . . . Push!

Before you were conceived
I wanted you.
Before you were born
I loved you.
Before you were an hour old
I would die for you.
This is the miracle of love.

—Maureen Hawkins

Susan Sarandon and Tim Robbins hold their baby in 1989. © Robert Sherbow/Timepix

This little soul really wants to be here, so it's meant to be.

—Susan Sarandon

My experience as a pregnant woman has shown me that the process of holding life within you changes you. For the pregnant woman the physical changes are numerous and humbling. The changes in the heart are greater.

—Julie Donovan Massey
De Pere, Wisconsin

The one universal joy any pregnant woman feels is the first time her baby kicks. It is exhilarating to feel this life growing inside of me. I feel very feminine and proud to be a woman, connected to all mothers who have experienced this joy. Even

Molly Hochstettler, barefoot and pregnant.

though my baby is unborn, her movements help me develop a bond with her. I want to hold and protect her. And I truly understand the strong mother-child bond that women have felt throughout history. As women, we are given the innate gift of nurturing. Pregnancy intensifies this quality and prepares us for our baby to be. When we are able to feel our babies move, this little miracle crystallizes into reality.

—Molly Hochstettler
South Bend, Indiana

I look forward to being a mom and hope that I can be as great a blessing to my child as my mom is to me.

—Cindy Edwards
Annapolis, Maryland

Forty-Week Transformation

By Beatriz Castillo de Vincent

I had left work earlier than usual. I was not feeling well and decided to go see the doctor. I suspected I was pregnant. When I saw her, she said that it was still too early, but gave me the name of a take-home pregnancy test and assured me that the results would be reliable. On my way home, I stopped by the pharmacy and bought the test. I was very excited and could not wait to find out if I was pregnant.

Right as I walked into the apartment, my husband called. It must have been around four or four-thirty local time. We were living in Prague, in the Czech Republic. He told me that something terrible was happening in New York. We had lived there for a few years. He proposed to marry me at the Brooklyn promenade overlooking the tip of the island of Manhattan. That place holds many cherished memories for both of us. We ended the conversation abruptly; he was at work and had to leave. He did not give me more details.

I turned on the television, to the only English-speaking channel that our cable service provided, just to see the video of the twin towers collapsing. At first I thought I was watching previews of a new-age movie but when I halfway realized what was happening something inside of me collapsed, too. I sat down. My thoughts were all scattered. I had friends living in the city. I myself had worked in a building nearby. I glanced at the plastic bag that contained the pregnancy test. I stared at it for some time and put it aside. It did not feel like the right moment to find out whether I was about to bring a little one into this scary world. I was afraid of the present and could not dare think of what the future might hold. For the next few days my husband and I were lost in a mournful haze.

Then something inside of me much stronger than fear and more scorching than pain, something deeper and hopeful, drove me to look ahead. After a day at work, I came home and took the pregnancy test. It was all written in Czech. I had to take out my dictionary to figure out exactly what it meant, partly because I did not understand the words and partly because I could not really believe what it said. I was pregnant.

I felt a mixture of awe, surprise, and disbelief. I was contemplating a mystery too deep to grasp and translate into a concrete expression. In the midst of this world's tragedy, I was being blessed. This new life was shedding light into my world and the world of my beloved ones. We held on to the promise of this baby as our source of joy and hope for a brighter future. I suddenly realized that life and love are stronger than anything, stronger than death. And with the hope came peace.

At that moment, my life began to undergo a complete yet subtle transformation, like all major changes in nature. My mother said it better than anyone: "You will change like a field for the harvest. All in you will breed life." Someone else was taking full possession of myself—not only my body, but also my thoughts, my moods, my feelings. Throughout the pregnancy I have been wrapped in some sort of cloud. My new forgetful and absentminded disposition has lulled me and sheltered me from my daily worries and the trivialities of my life. I catch myself laughing more often. The things that used to bother and upset me have assumed their real dimension and insignificance. But at the same time, the cloud has lifted me up so I could take a wider look at the world and feel more deeply for it.

I wondered what the pregnant women in Afghanistan were feeling while their country was being bombed, how they struggled to get to the Pakistani shelters to deliver their babies. When I glanced at the lists of foods and nutrients I had to take on a daily basis, I wondered how women in Africa or India manage to bring their babies into the world. As I sat with my swollen legs at work, I often thought of my home, of Mexico. My thoughts went to the single mothers who have to work throughout their entire pregnancies, take trams, buses, and subways late into the evening, find their way through the masses of people moving about. Then I thought of the pregnant women whose husbands were absent and the desperation and hopelessness of those who seek refuge in abortion. It is hard to describe the aches and pains that my heart was beginning to feel for all those around me.

I realized how absolutely impossible it was for me to be in control of this overwhelming world surrounding me and my child. With so many changes in my body, knowing that the life inside of me was still so very fragile, I felt so vulnerable that I had to cling to someone higher, someone wiser and loving, to nurture and protect me and the little one inside. In this sense, I was also becoming a baby. Nothing I had gone through so far had required me to experience such a total letting go and a dependency on my God. Nothing had required such strength in my faith.

It is frightening for us, the professional women of the

twenty-first century, to have to relinquish control. But it is liberating, similar to the sense of relief when, after the first months of pregnancy, you finally slide into a pair of roomy maternity pants!

Becoming aware of my own vulnerability has also made me feel closer to my husband and able to recognize the importance of his love in my life. I am learning to rely more on him and to honor our relationship. I also feel much closer to my girlfriends and feel a real kinship with any mother, especially anyone expecting.

So, as my belly gets larger, the nights shorter, and the trips to the rest room more frequent, I have to let go. Let go of my old concept of time. Now I measure life in weeks. Let go of my job, my personal plans, my old figure, my favorite clothes, my unhealthy habits. At one point, after an unexpected bleeding sent me to bed rest, I even had to let go of my desire to have a baby. In this having to let go, my will wrestles and rebels. I am afraid of the pain of labor, of losing my mind in the delivery room or afterward. I am afraid of the sleepless and stressful nights ahead of us. I am afraid of what it really means when my older friends look at me with condescending eyes and say, "Just wait and see, your life will *never* be the same again." What about *my* future? What about *my* life? Am I really to be someone else's *mom?*

Yet I feel so special, so unique. When I sense the baby kicking and growing inside my body, I feel a deep joy. In my discreet and seemingly insignificant life at home, I finally feel at peace. I am a vessel. I am the carrier of a miracle. I am an instrument through which life and love will flow. And this has given more meaning to my life than anything else I have ever experienced. As I wait for the forty weeks to pass by, I can only dream of what it will be like to finally hold this baby in my arms.

Beatriz Castillo de Vincent, born and raised in Mexico, now lives in Munich, Germany.

❧

During pregnancy, I understood the continuity of life and death, that my body was a city and a landscape, and that I had personally discovered the moral equivalent of war. During the final stage of labor I felt like a hero, an Olympic athlete, a figure out of Pindar, at whom a stadium should be heaving garlands.

—Alicia Ostriker

Princeton, New Jersey

What is true about giving birth is that it is miraculous. . . . For one thing, though my stomach was huge and the baby constantly causing turbulence within it, I did not believe a baby, a person, would come out of me. I mean, look what had gone in. But there she was, coming out, a long black curling lock of hair the first part to be seen, followed by nearly ten pounds of— a human being.

—Alice Walker

At the moment of birth, I felt myself drown in a dark tunnel; as ego flickered out, something else sustained me. I felt both accomplished and exquisitely passive, a collaborator in something that was going to happen with or without my consent. A baby was placed on my chest, a baby with wildly rolling eyes. He clamped on to the nearest breast, a tug I could feel right down to my womb. . . .

I inspected my son. A swirl of dark hair. A high, wrinkled brow, which I immediately attributed to tension rather than his protracted stay in the birth canal. Strong features, wide hands, abominable-snowman feet. While I craned my neck to look at him, a total stranger stitched me up. My body, I had learned, was an unsung genius. It was in cahoots with something bigger. This was sobering—a loss of conscious control, and a gaining of some deeper allegiances.

—Marni Jackson
Toronto, Canada

On the day my twins were born, I got up before dawn, showered, put on just a touch of mascara, and sat on the end of the bed to wait. . . . I remember every detail—a day like this is lifted from the rest; it stands alone, etched in light.

—Mia Farrow

Labor of Love

By Louise Erdrich

Rocking, breathing, groaning, mouthing circles of distress, laughing, whistling, pounding, wavering, digging, pulling, pushing—labor is the most involuntary work we do. My body gallops to these rhythms. I'm along for the ride, at times in some control and at others dragged along as if foot-caught in a stirrup. I don't have much to do at first but breathe, accept ice chips, make jokes—in fear and pain my family makes jokes. That's how we deal with what we can't change, how we show our courage.

Birth is intensely spiritual and physical all at once. The contractions do not stop. There is no giving up this physical prayer. The person who experiences birth with the closest degree of awareness is the mother—but not only am I physically programmed to forget the experience to some degree (our brains "extinct" fear, we are all programmed to forget pain over time, and hormones seem to assist), I am overwhelmed by what is happening to me. I certainly can't take notes, jot down my sensations, or even have them with any perspective for a while. And then, once our baby is actually born, the experience of labor, even at its most intense, is eclipsed by the presence of an infant.

The first part of labor feels, to me anyway, like dance exercises—slow stretches that become only slightly painful as a muscle is pulled to its limit. After each contraction, the feeling subsides. The contractions move in longer waves, one after another, closer and closer together until a sea of physical sensation washes and then crashes over. In the beginning I breathe in concentration, watching Michael's eyes. I feel myself slip beneath the waves as they roar over, cresting just above my head. I duck every time the contraction peaks. As the hours pass and one wave builds on another there are times the undertow grabs me. I struggle, slammed to the bottom, unable to gather the force of nerve for the next. Thrown down, I rely on animal fierceness, swim back, surface, breathe, and try to stay open, willing. Staying open and willing is difficult. Very often in labor one must fight the instinct to resist pain and instead embrace it, move toward it, work with what hurts the most.

The waves come faster. Charlotte asks me to keep breathing *yes, yes.* To say yes instead of shuddering in refusal. Whether I am standing on the earth or not, whether I am moored to the dock, whether I remember who I am, whether I am mentally prepared, whether I am going to float beneath or ride above, the waves pound in. At shorter intervals, crazy now, electric, in storms they wash. Sometimes I'm gone. I've poured myself into some deeper fissure below the sea only to be dragged forth, hair streaming. During transition, as the baby is ready to be pushed out into life, the waves are no longer made of water, but neons so brilliant I gasp in shock and flourish my arms, letting the colors explode from my fingertips in banners, in ribbons, in iridescent trails—of pain, it is true, unendurable sometimes, and yet we do endure.

Every birth is profoundly original and yet plotted a billion times, too many times. Some push once, some don't push at all, some push in pleasure, some not and some, like me, for hours. We wreak havoc, make animal faces, ugly bare-toothed faces, go red, go darker, whiter, stranger, turn to bears. We choke spouses, beat nurses, beg them, beg doctors, weep and focus. It is our work, our body's work that is involved in its goodness. For, even though it wants at times to lie down and quit, the body is an honest hardworking marvel that gives everything to this task.

At last, with the birth of each daughter, Michael and I experience a certainty of apprehension, a sensation so profound that I feel foggy brained attempting to describe how, in the first moment after birth, the actual being of a new person appears.

We touch our baby's essential mystery. The three of us are soul to soul.

Louise Erdrich is the author of *The Blue Jay's Dance* and a mother of three.

❧

It wasn't simply the surprise of seeing who it was that had been inside me, upside down and underwater, or that she was as purple and pointy as a crayon—it was the way my daughter looked at me, imprinting me in her brain. She seemed to look right into me, as if she knew me. It was the most terrifying and beautiful moment in my life.

—Elissa Schappell
New York, New York

There is nothing on earth like the moment of seeing one's first baby. Men scale other heights, but there is no height like this simple one, occurring continuously throughout the ages in musty bedrooms, in palaces, in caves and desert places.

—Katharine Trevelyan

The baby was born, and in the instant I laid eyes on him, wrinkled and ugly like the babies I always had ignored, I fell in love. He was red and warm and I held him on my breast. He was perfect.

—Helen Winternitz
Long Island, New York

I can't get over the miracle of giving birth. It was as if the sun had opened up. I became free.

—Jane Fonda

When a child who has been conceived in love is born to a man and woman, the joy of that birth sings throughout the universe.

—Madeleine L'Engle

Interlude ✑

Casey was six weeks old. I would get dents in my knees from the texture of the living-room rug as I knelt watching him sleep in his basket. This gazing was a full-time job. . . . I discovered a new meaning in "Every Breath You Take." Every breath you take, I'll be watching you.

In every other way, life was turning out differently than I had imagined, but here was this large, silk-skinned, clever-mouthed baby who triggered such straightforward love. All he did was eat, sleep, and screw his face up in uncivilized ways, and yet to my eyes he was mesmerizing in every detail, from the wide, square hands with their shocking newborn strength, to his creased, articulate feet, unblunted by shoes. Each movement fascinated, like the undulation of a snake or the slowed-down flight of a bird—I never ran out of wonder. The complexity of the adult he would become, the most convoluted thought he would ever think seemed to be already there in his expression, clear and abbreviated. I understood what it meant to feast on the sight of someone.

—Marni Jackson
Toronto, Canada

Baby Bliss

In the sheltered simplicity of the first days after a baby is born, one sees again the magical closed circle. The miraculous sense of two people existing only for each other.

—Anne Morrow Lindbergh

I never knew real passion until I had my first child. The smell that emanated from the deep recesses of her neck literally intoxicated me. I would lean over that crib and bury my face in her neck and inhale her smell until my back gave out or I began to hyperventilate. I don't wonder how it is that wild animal mothers can always identify the smell of their own offspring, differentiating them from the smells of all seemingly identical babies. The smell of your own offspring is more real and potent than any other sensory experience.

—Dena Shottenkirk

It's hard to have a dark mood with a gurgling, delightful, cherubic baby kissing you and hugging you.

—Jane Seymour

Actress Jane Seymour holding
daughter Katie at poolside.
© Ann Clifford/DMI/Timepix

What feeling is so nice as child's hand in yours? So small, so soft and warm, like a kitten huddling in the shelter of your clasp.
—Marjorie Holmes

I had a tiny baby, whom I loved taking care of. He was adorable. I loved the smell and feel of him, his helplessness and total dependence on me. I loved him so much (as happened later with all my babies) that I thought my heart would burst.
—Rosalynn Carter

Maternal Bondage

By Mary Kay Blakely

The first clue, certainly, that motherhood was going to be far more provocative and complicated than anything I'd imagined came the night I went into labor with my first son, as Howard began coaching me in the deep-breathing techniques we'd practiced in our natural childbirth classes. In 1974 enthusiasm among our friends in Fort Wayne for all things natural approached an almost religious fervor.

According to our Lamaze instructor that winter, my body was supposed to "self-anesthetize" during labor and delivery, allowing me to remain wholly alert for the miracle of birth. She assured our class of hefty, plural-bodied women that our cervix muscles would become "naturally numb" as they swelled and stretched, and deep breathing would turn the final explosions of pain into "manageable discomfort." This description turned out to be as accurate as, say, a steward advising passengers aboard the *Titanic* to prepare for a brisk but bracing swim. If my self-anesthesia took at all, it packed the power of two baby aspirin.

Before I lost my innocence in the maternity wing of Parkview Hospital that winter, I imagined facing my biological destiny as calmly as the natural mothers in the home birth movies, issuing a low moan now and then but never screaming insensibly or savagely biting the hands of the gentle attending fathers—all bearded, naturally. In a cool ninety minutes flat, the home birth moms went from calisthenic huffing to tears of joy to cogent monologues about birth as a spiritual experience. According to eyewitnesses, my own performance as a saint was brief.

After six hours of unremitting pain, I was nearly blind with sweat and exhaustion when the transforming moment arrived a few minutes before dawn on February 24, 1974. Looking down on my chest where someone had placed the wet, squirmy mass I dimly recognized as my son, I raised my head to offer a limp welcoming smile and immediately passed out. Both of my sons, as it turned out, were required to spend their first hours in the brave new world without me, as I struggled to regain consciousness in another room. This surreal relationship might have been the best introduction they could have had to living with a writer—but it was hardly intentional. From day one, it was clear I'd never be one of the movie moms. Both of my sons would be obliged to live with the real thing.

"After going through this once, whatever made you decide to do it four more times?" I asked my mother when I called that morning with news of her first grandson. She laughed. "You'll be surprised," she said, "how much that baby boy will make you forgive and forget." She chose not to mention just then, on my fragile first day, how much this baby would also shake me down to the barest truths about myself, as her own firstborn son had, exposing an unimaginable capacity for love and rage I would have the rest of my life. There would have been no point in her telling me the full, harrowing details of this life-altering journey then. With this son and, as she correctly anticipated, another one a mere eighteen months later, I was already committed. Although none of us could know how the strands of biology, culture, and fate would spin out of control in the years ahead, the web was begun.

My mother was right, too, about the general amnesty a newborn is granted after the ordeal of birth. When the nurse came into my room with the tiny creature responsible for the violent seizures the night before, now quietly subdued and bound in a blue receiving blanket, mercy and gratitude tied a hard knot in my throat. I thought Ryan Blake, four hours old, was beauty itself. His pictures from this period reveal that, in fact, he was puffy-eyed and nearly bald, his chubby face registering the same blank amusement Oliver Hardy might have worn as an infant. That morning, however, I saw only his uncanny resemblance to the airbrushed perfection of a Gerber baby. Here he was—dreamed about and yearned for—an actual son. My son? Our son. A living, breathing, hungry, wanting, healthy, gorgeous son.

Mary Kay Blakely is the author of *American Mom* and the mother of two sons.

✑

Curly, blond-haired Leslie with straight, dark-haired William.

I always thought my child would have curly blond hair because I have a mass of curly blond hair. It's distinctive, and people often comment on it. On the street I'd see a little girl in a pink dress with a thick tangle of ringlets, and I'd smile.

But my son, William, has a shock of straight, silky, dark brown, almost-black hair. As if to highlight my folly, he was born with a full head of hair, making his hair one of his most distinctive features. It's long, too, covering his ears and neck, and it sticks straight up all over his head. My husband and I smile when anyone first meets William because inevitably the first thing said is "Look at that hair!"

Now I can't picture William with curly blond hair. He wouldn't be William, and William is perfect. In fact, I can't think of anything so completely unimportant as the color of William's hair. I once thought that William's hair would have meaning. Now only William has meaning. I couldn't love him any more than I do.

> —Leslie Nichols
> Mayport, Florida

When Chelsea Victoria Clinton lay in my arms for the first time, I was overwhelmed by the love and responsibility I felt for her. Despite all the books I had read, all the children I had studied and advocated for, nothing had prepared me for the sheer miracle of her being.

> —Hillary Rodham Clinton

I saw pure love when my son looked at me, and I knew that I had to make a good life for the two of us.

> —Suzanne Somers

She was a beautiful baby. She blew shining bubbles of sound. She loved motion, loved light, loved color and music and textures. She would lie on the floor in her blue overalls patting the surface so hard in ecstasy her hands and feet would blur. She was a miracle to me.

> —Tillie Olsen
> Berkeley, California

Her smile was like a rainbow after a sudden storm.

> —Colette

Three-Month Reprieve

By Anne Lamott

There are huge changes every day now. Maybe there always were, but I was too tired to notice. His main activities currently are nursing, foot sucking, making raspberries and bubbles, and chewing on his Odie doll's ear. We were sitting out beneath the moon again, nursing, and it occurred to me that someday he will stare at the full moon and know the word for it.

Things are getting better now. They've been easier for a month. People kept telling me that I just had to hold on until the end of the third month and everything would get easier. I always thought they were patronizing me or trying to keep me from scrounging up cab fare to the bridge. But I remember a month ago, when he turned three months and one or two days—it was like the baby looked at his little watch calendar and said with a bit of surprise, "Oh, for Chrissakes, it's been three months already—time to chill out a little." He sleeps every night, and doesn't cry or gritch very often, and just in general seems to be enjoying his stay a little bit more. It's much better. I'm much better. This guy I know who is really nuts and really spiritual said the other day, "My mind is a bad neighborhood that I try not to go into alone." That pretty much says it for me in the first three months.

My friend Michelle calls the first three months the fourth trimester.

Another thing I notice is that I'm much less worried all

the time—a lot of things are no big deal now, whereas in the beginning everything was. For instance, now Sam can go for a few days without pooping, or can poop ten times in one day, without my automatically thinking he has some terrible intestinal blockage or deformity that will require a colostomy and that will make trying to get him into day care a living hell.

He's becoming so grown-up before my very eyes. It's so painful. I want him to stay this age forever.

I look at him all the time and think, "Where'd you come from?" as if out of the blue, some Bouvier puppy came to live here with me and the kitty. I don't really know how it happened. It seems like I was just sitting around reading a book, and what book it was I can't remember, and then all of a sudden, here he is, sucking on his foot and his Odie doll's ear.

He has this beautiful hand gesture where, when he's nursing, he reaches back with his free hand to touch and lightly pat the crown of his head, and it looks exactly like he's checking to see if his bald spot is exposed.

Anne Lamott is the best-selling author of *Operating Instructions* and *Traveling Mercies*.

❧

Nine months now—he's been out in the world for as long as he was within me. And he's become a part of everything around him as much as he is a part of me. He's taken possession—the cats, the furniture, his toys, his clothes, the music he hears, his daddy's heartbeat. Last night he laughed and laughed as I imitated the gibberish sounds his friend Charlie makes—a kind *of Samurai exclamation in response to small surprises. After we went to sleep, I held within me an almost uneasy sense of lurking euphoria, of the sort you have when you've received a large gift, or extraordinary news, or a confession of love from someone you thought to be indifferent. It's not those things themselves that cause the euphoria, but the aftermath during which you briefly forget what it is that's gotten into you, and then you remember. There's some sort of chemical that's injected into my bloodstream in that instant between forgetting and remembering. His laughter brought that about, and I can't put into words the relief I felt when I remembered that it was him, my boy, my burden, who could make me feel this way. Not a new harpsichord, $10,000 in stock, a job offer, or someone else's intoxicated stare—just him in his long nine months devouring the air around him.*

—Vivian Montgomery
Cleveland, Ohio

Diana Ross with daughters in 1976. © Bettmann/Corbis

For me, being a working mom is a blessing. I think my career was a positive force in raising my three daughters. I like to think it made me a better mother because since I was satisfied in my own life, I could encourage them to follow their personal destinies. I also think I was a positive role model in showing them how to balance commitments between work and family.

—Diana Ross

As my children grow older, I feel it's extremely important to make them understand just how much Mommy loves her work. I want them to realize that through hard work and a good education, they, too, can become anything they choose. I want my daughters to grow up respecting their working mom, to be proud of me and view me as their role model. But that won't happen if they feel in any way that my career detracted from my role as their mother and their biggest source of support and understanding—and that's exactly why balancing your job and your family is so incredibly important.

—Mary Lou Retton

Being a mother is another life. You're at home and you're with your child, playing with the toys, changing diapers. Life becomes all about the real stuff; the rest isn't as important. But don't get me wrong: to come back and do a record was more fun than ever because I've never felt as strong. I feel like a complete person.

—Celine Dion

FIVE

From Cubicle to Playground and in Between

There is no job I wanted to be better at than raising and loving my three daughters. The rewards have no ending.

—Pat Ertel

Tampa, Florida

It's easy to lose sight of the larger perspective when we're caught up in daily life—signing permission slips, making lunches, teaching our children to be kind to one another. It doesn't always feel as if we're doing anything truly profound. And yet with each kiss, with each lesson, we are doing the work of the ages.

—Denise Roy
Santa Clara, California

Enduring Boredom

By Gayle Boss

My youngest child started kindergarten this week— Tuesdays, Thursdays, and every other Friday, all day. For the first time in ten years I am alone in my own house on some weekdays. Ten weekdays a month, on average, though holidays, teacher in-service days, and child sick days subtract from that number. I have counted the days, I have waited for the days, I have made delicious plans for them. But now that they're here I find I can't dive into them without a look back at the place where I've wandered for a decade of my life—a land of Uselessness, a Sinai wilderness in the suburbs.

Anyone who's cared for children and a home knows it's not, literally, useless work. There is an endless list of things to do that make life possible and, depending on how the tasks are done, more or less pleasant: food to grow or buy and prepare, clothes and dishes to wash, beds to make, bathrooms to scrub, dirt (of all kinds) to sweep up, fights to settle, lessons in sharing, table manners, and personal hygiene to give . . . and give and give. I've often felt like Sisyphus, pushing the boulder up the slope, falling asleep at the top sprawled over the rock, only to wake and find myself, again, at the bottom of the hill. And no one there to rally me with a pep talk and a pat on the back. Almost never do those hungry mouths and sweet-skinned bodies say thank you.

But they do grow. Sometimes they even exhibit manners in public. The home, lived in, cared for, acquires a certain character, like a comfortable old sweater that smells of its wearer and holds her shape; loved ones return to it. There are moments the caregiver and homemaker sees and feels some good outcome. But in the day to day, day after day, they are rare, these moments of small, subtle reward. There are long stretches of unmarked territory between watering holes.

At age thirty-four I made the choice to let four years of graduate-level education and twelve years of workplace skills lie dormant while my children were at home. I could have worked, at least part time, and I don't fault mothers

Gayle Boss with her two sons.

who do. There have been weeks when I ached to be back among them, walking out the door toward some work useful to the world outside my four walls, walking back in with a paycheck to ease the monthly pinch and to buy me treats. Money, too, to contribute to good ministries. But from the first week of my first child's life I have known with a clarity that's come to me only rarely, at a few life crossroads, that I was being directed—commanded even, the voice was that insistent—to stay put with crying babies and demanding preschoolers. To plod through the never-ending round of domestic chores. To endure the boredom.

Looking back, I see I needed remedial instruction in how to work. For twelve years I had worked for money, I'd worked to see the successes stack up, I'd worked to avoid others' disapproval. When I came home from the hospital with my first son I found I was a disappeared person from the places where decisions are made and accomplishments made public. It was baby and me at home, alone, me asking what, now, would make me feel worthwhile. When the baby wasn't crying it was deathly still.

Nine months into the tedium of full-time mothering, I was sitting slumped on the edge of a sandbox in a neighborhood park, watching my son plow his fingers and toes through dirty sand, when another woman plopped her baby next to mine and asked if I was new to the neighborhood. She invited me to a neighborhood playgroup that met every Friday morning. "Socialization opportunities for the children" was the public justification we gave for the group. But all the mothers knew that the real reason we rushed together Friday after Friday and saw each other in smaller groupings in between was to relax in a sisterhood of women wounded in our self-confidence and uncertain about our worth and identity in a land that offered us no rewards other than lip service.

Finally I had joined up with my tribe. I was not alone in that Wilderness of Uselessness. From then on I leaned on and learned from other mothers, those of the Friday morning playgroup and others they led me to. I learned by listening to their stories and telling mine. Listening to their fears, their disappointments, their barely held hopes; telling mine. From the wisest ones I heard kitchen table poems; striking insights about Who We Are and Why We're Here, insights gained from care-full attention focused on the ordinary: the bulge of a child's belly, jam smeared on the wall, a favorite toy lost. These women were the ones whose addiction to approval and reward had begun to ease. The taskmasters' voices were fainter for them. When they gave themselves to the wilderness life and its tedious chores they began to hear something else: the silence was laced with a music like heartbeats; out of the mouths of babes they heard wisdom, they glimpsed heaven.

So taken was I with their hearing and seeing of what I thought was the boring ordinary I began to imitate their way of doing daily domestic work: slow down, try to do just one thing at a time, do it with your eyes and ears and heart open. It's taken me a decade to learn these basics, and mostly I fall far short of what's possible. I draw hope from noticing that even in failure my desire to live this wide-awake way keeps growing more fervent.

Domestic tedium, like any desert, has tuned my eyes and ears to the subtle, the hidden, to the still, small voice that directs from within: *See this child in the tub, flushed and reaching for you? This is the Presence in the present. This is holy ground, and it is more than enough. Be here.*

Standing now at the edge of the river, the gaping mother-of-small-children wilderness mostly behind me, I'm balking. I not sure I want to dive in and swim to the other side, to the banks of the bustling, purpose-full land. My toes are wet; I'm wading in; it's time to cross and I know it, as certainly as I knew when it was time to stay put. It's not so much that I'm afraid to face how incompetent I've become in the world of (computerized!) public labor. I'm more afraid of being swept up into the whooshing rush of Important Work, of being intoxicated by Usefulness. I'm afraid I'll lose, fragile as it is, my wilderness hearing, the ears that can hear, now and then, in a small child's questions, the Creator's smile.

Gayle Boss is a freelance writer living in Grand Rapids, Michigan, with her husband and two sons.

꙳

Recently, as I was grating apple and mashing up banana, I experienced an odd moment of realization: even my most glorious corporate moments from days gone by do not begin to equal the happiness I feel performing a mundane chore for my sixteen-month-old little princess—Anna Olivia.

I had to stop and think about it. Did I really believe this fleeting thought? After all, I reminded myself, I have experienced several memorial moments working for a prestigious international law firm and then the United Nations. And let's not forget that I found new motherhood to be so encompassing and exhausting—for the first six months of Anna Olivia's existence I hardly slept due to her difficult (or should I say nonexistent) sleep pattern; finding the right moment to take a shower

Donna Smith with daughter Anna
Olivia.

*was an ordeal, and just reading the paper (something I had
once taken for granted) was now a luxury!*

*Indeed, I admitted to myself as I grated more apple that I
needed, I missed my working life as an international lawyer and
the freedom and intellectual stimulation that goes along with it
(not to mention the salary). Life was so easy back then! And, in
retrospect, so empty.*

*It is impossible to accurately describe the highs of mother-
hood. They are emotions that must be experienced to be truly
understood. Suffice to say, however, the highs are like nothing I
have ever known. Listening to my little girl's giggles as we watch*
The Wiggles *on TV; the smiles we share as we rearrange her
various teddies; the pride I feel as she pronounces new words
daily; and the total unconditional, innocent love that radiates
from her as we go about our day cannot be matched.*

*So, yes, my moment of realization crystallized into accept-
ing that motherhood is more satisfying that anything else I've*

ever accomplished. The corporate world may make the economy go around, the United Nations may resolve international conflicts, but motherhood—and proper mothering—comes before all that. For we not only create but shape the next generation.

         —Donna Smith
         Melbourne, Australia

I remember the exact moment I felt myself breaking ranks with the Feminist Movement. I had decided to stay home—a choice. I was married to a man who woke up in the middle of the night to help with nursing, who made Saturday "Daddy Day" from the word "go." And then the act of treason. The moment of truth.

It started with a question posed to my then eighteen-month-old daughter: "Would you like to bake some cookies?" Wasting a master of divinity degree on cookie baking. An ordained clergywoman—baking cookies at home. So many women had endured so much humiliation. And here I was, proving the bad, good old boys right.

My daughter and I made the chocolate chip cookie dough together. Major flour spill. She licked the bowl clean. We baked the cookies, and it smelled just like my mom's.

I gave her the first homemade cookie she had ever eaten. She bit big into the cookie and beamed. Smiling the biggest little girl smile. It was delicious, warm, sweet, satisfying. Full of sunbeam.

I beamed back. I had made my daughter very happy.

And as I surrendered to her unadulterated happiness, I knew. It was the beginning of the end.

Giving into her happiness also meant giving in to "the Mommy Track."

I like being a mom. I also like working. But there is a time for every purpose under heaven. A time to achieve prestigious goals. A time to shake the money tree. And a time to bake cookies.

—Sarah Woods

Annapolis, Maryland

If you bungle raising your children, nothing much else matters in life.

—Jackie Onassis

Before my first daughter was born, I taught school. It was hard giving up that career and the extra pay. I thought that mothers who worked really had it great, and I marveled at how they could juggle their time as mothers and businesswomen. As it turned out, staying home was the most precious and wonderful experience of my life. I was there to witness every stage of their

Jackie and Caroline in 1960.
© Alfred Eisenstaedt/Timepix

growth: first bath, first smile, first tooth, first illness, first word, first step, first day of school, and all the other firsts. I wouldn't trade it for anything. I am really the lucky one!

—Peg Hall

Beavercreek, Ohio

I looked on child rearing not only as a work of love and duty but as a profession that was fully as interesting and challenging as any honorable profession in the world and one that demanded the best that I could bring to it.

—Rose Kennedy

To nourish children and raise them against odds is in any time, any place, more valuable than to fix bolts in cars or design nuclear weapons.

—Marilyn French

A Woman's Place Is Everywhere

By Cokie Roberts

Just a few weeks before she died at the age of ninety-seven, former senator Margaret Chase Smith wrote an introduction to the book *Outstanding Women Members to Congress.* " 'Where is the proper place of women?' is a question I have often been asked," she begins. "The quizzers have asked this question ambitiously, defiantly, hopefully—and just plain inquisitively. But it has been asked so many times in so many ways and by so many types of people that, of necessity, my answer has had to transcend the normal and understandable prejudice that a woman might have. My answer is short and simple—woman's proper place is everywhere. Individually it is where the particular woman is happiest and best fitted—in the home as wives and mothers; in organized civic, business and professional groups; in industry and business, both management and labor; and in government and politics. Generally, if there is any proper place for women today, it is that of alert and responsible citizens in the fullest sense of the word."

Because our communities and our country need us just as the children do, the country requires the services of women soldiers and politicians and businesswomen and clubwomen and consumer and civil rights activists and women helping other women get off welfare and nurses and nuns. The country needs us to be sisters and aunts and friends and mothers and daughters and wives first in the literal sense and then in the figurative one—sisters to society, caretakers.

Women can complain forever about how our devotion to those roles is not remunerated, that society doesn't compensate us for our nurturing. And frankly, I don't think we'll ever solve that problem. If we want public recognition and financial reward, we will continue to have to "do it all." But that's not such a terrible thing. One piece of advice for young women: Don't worry about it so much. There are times when life's emotionally and physically exhausting, and times when sleep deprivation seems likely to do you in, but you'll make it. Women are tough. We've managed to keep all the balls in the air for a very long time.

These are issues I've been puzzling about most of my adult life. Recently I unearthed a journal where I occasionally jotted down thoughts while we were living in Greece. I found an entry from twenty-one years ago, when I was thirty-three years old and contemplating our family's next move.

"No one writes about women like me, and we probably form a large group, who daily make the choice about our career, family, etc. It's not a one-time decision, but a continual one. And we can get so trapped by any alternative—the pure kid, pure work or balance. So can a man, of course, but in nothing like the same way."

That was a long time ago, and so far I haven't gotten trapped. I've been blessed with a gloriously happy marriage, two fabulous kids now safely launched, the many joys of family and friendship, and a fine, fulfilling career. By living on this earth long enough, I've learned that clichés are clichés because they are true. It's true that you'll only have one opportunity to witness your baby's first step, to hold your dying sister's hand, to see your mother credentialed by the Pope, to hold your mother-in-law as she learns of her husband's death, to celebrate thirty years with your husband. There will always be another job.

So what is a woman's place? For most women it's many places, different places at different times. For almost all women, it's the place of nurturer, whether for the planet or one small creature on it. We learned it from our mothers, both in word and in deed, we teach it to our daughters in the knowledge that they must carry on the culture and care for it. . . . From that continuity they will derive the strength to make their place wherever they think it should be.

Cokie Roberts is a radio and television news analyst, author, and mother of two.

❧

Motherhood is a roughed-out roadway with the tours and de-tours each and every family takes in order to survive. The roadway is littered with missing school shoes and forgotten school assignments; with appliances that have been taken apart and "fixed"; with drums in the basement and guitars on the roof; with broken swing sets, fenderless bikes, and a thousand Matchbox cars; damp hair and sticky fingers; with tears and hugs and kisses; and many broken hearts. That is why every mother needs to feel free to navigate that roadway on her own terms.

—Eileen McCafferty

DiFranco

Philadelphia, Pennsylvania

To be sure, it's not always easy. I worry when I say no to a story that requires a lot of travel. Will this be the final straw for my bosses? Each time I turn down an assignment because it conflicts with a child's special performance or a soccer game, I hold my breath for their reaction. Will they fire me now? In my desire to be at home and hands-on, I have made some pretty reckless decisions.

—Maria Shriver

After my daughter Molly's birth, I returned to work and was burning the candle at both ends, given the demands of motherhood and a full-time job in the newspaper business. I knew there must be a secret for maintaining the energy I needed to do both jobs well and yet remaining calm until life settled into a routine at home and at work. So I called the wife of the chairman of the company where I worked and asked her how she did it, with five boys and two girls. Her response: "Never sit down. If you sit down, you'll relax and you won't be able to get back up!" That was precisely the answer I needed, and it actually works! I should know—I've been following her advice for almost eighteen years.

—Martha Flanagan
Cincinnati, Ohio

I did it [raised the children] ad hoc, like any working mother does. Every woman who's got a household knows exactly what I did. I did it on a minute-to-minute basis. . . . There was never a place I worked, or a time I worked, that my children did not interrupt me, no matter how trivial—because it was never trivial to them.

—Toni Morrison

Interlude

He laughed today for the first time, when Julie from upstairs was dangling her bracelets above his head while I was changing his diaper. His laughter was like little bells. Then there was the clearest silence, a hush, before total joyous pandemonium broke out between Julie and me. Then we both stared almost heartbrokenly into his face. I thought of Wallace Stevens' "Thirteen Ways of Looking at a Blackbird," verse five:

> I do not know which to prefer,
> The beauty of inflections
> Or the beauty of innuendoes,
> The blackbird whistling
> Or just after.

> —Anne Lamott

SIX

Miracles, Milestones, and More

There is no doubt that these first things are magical, that you hunch over the changing table waiting for another smile, that you shriek, "You rolled over!" as though the next step will be the Nobel or the presidency, that a first step is like watching the history of human civilization from small fishy things to Neanderthals unravel in one instant before your eyes.

—Anna Quindlen

In the white room, over weeks and months, buoyed by minuscule but ongoing success, I tried whatever entered my mind to catch his eye and hold it; I bought lipstick and eye shadow in every color, I painted dots, stripes, patterns, all over my face, I

Actress Mia Farrow reading to her adoptive Vietnamese daughter Lark and others. © Alfred Eisenstaedt/Timepix

covered it with tin foil, then with Saran Wrap, I blew smoke out of my mouth, blew bubble-gum bubbles, crinkled cellophane between my teeth, ate carrots, potato chips, I wore gloves, I lugged in pots of water to splash in, I sang, whistled, tickled, and clucked. I had seen my baby son smile at crinkling cellophane and at the crunch of autumn leaves underfoot. Finally, now, he smiled at me.

—Mia Farrow

He smiled the other day for the first time, and I was running around the room going, "Oh, my God! Oh, my God!" I was gushing more than Mount Saint Helens.

—Janet Hubert Whitten

Nikolai is standing on his own for the first time today. As I watch him and clap wildly, I am filled with that mixture of happiness and sadness peculiar to mothers.

—Gail Greiner

New York, New York

Every day is a milestone.

—Ricki Lake

Mama

By Therese J. Borchard

Last night my son spoke his first words.

At approximately eight o'clock in the evening, in between bites of creamed spinach and strained squash, my-nine-month old looks intently into my eyes and utters two

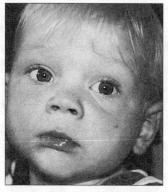

David a few days before speaking his first words.

syllables that will forever alter my purpose in life and give every waking hour of my day new meaning.

"Ma . . . ma . . ." he says, straining to join his upper and lower lips to form the consonant that I have been so diligently training him to say.

At first I doubt myself and look for confirmation to my husband, who is too busy recharging the camcorder batteries to give me a reassuring glance. We weren't expecting great things to happen tonight. Only a half hour prior to this miracle, I was griping about the thirty things I was unable to accomplish today with a fussy baby on my hands.

"Were you able to get to the bank?" my husband asked me as I unloaded the groceries from the trunk of the car and he microwaved frozen chili for supper with the relaxing background noise of a not-yet-boy-but-older-than-a-baby's temper tantrum.

"Ma . . . ma . . ." little David repeats, as tears trickle down my face and my heart flutters like the first time my husband told me he loved me.

By now the handyman of the house is catching this all through the lens of the camcorder, as if that will preserve the precious innocence of this stage, freezing this joyous moment so that we can digest it in small servings, like the big batch of chili we are reheating for the third time.

But these memories can't be unthawed. They only happen once.

We may replay them for years to come on our big-screen TV or computer monitor, but I won't be able to wipe the strained squash from my baby's chin or pick up his Binki covered with dog hair from the floor.

Fortunately there will be new tapes to play, of Little League games and prom dates, of first steps and college graduations. But he will only say the word *Mama* once for the very first time.

"Ma . . . ma," my bright-eyed cherub says, the word becoming clearer still.

It is now the third time he has spoken this, his first word, the most beautiful word in the English language.

Cameraman Eric and I are still in shock.

Then the sensitive guy takes a rest room break and the rational ego of a man takes over filming this historical moment.

"I thought he was supposed to say 'Dada' first," says Eric.

The professionals—everyone from the pediatrician to fellow parents at the park—told us that. Then they would pat my shoulder and tell me not to feel bad when it happens.

I should have known better than to listen to them. David has followed his own schedule for every milestone, confusing the experts every step of the way. He is more interested in learning how to walk than to crawl. He prefers an adult glass to bottles or sippy-cups, and I expect his molars to protrude before his two front teeth.

"Mama," says my little boy, as goose bumps form on my arms and in my soul. This word, his first word, is permanently etched on the contours of my heart, directing my body, mind, and spirit toward the destiny of motherhood.

There's no feeling on earth like the twist of the heart at that moment when a tiny youngster links that syllable, Ma, with the face of its mother. A connection is formed, and whether it evolves into the name Mom or Mama or Mother, it is a name that is as common as breath itself—and as unique as each set of two hearts it links.

—Barbara Johnson

Most children's first words are "Mama" or "Daddy." Mine were "Do I have to use my own money?"

—Erma Bombeck

Potty Training by the Book

By Jana Riess

It was supposed to be so easy. We had read The Book, you see. This book promised that our child would be completely potty-trained in less than a day. It claimed that after utilizing its methods, our daughter would never have accidents. We would sail merrily through life, free of our cumbersome and squeaky diaper bag, secretly laughing at other parents and wondering why they worried so much about the potty.

It didn't quite work out that way. The first clue that we might be in trouble came from Amazon.com, where customer reviews are often fair indicators of the usefulness or relevance of a particular book. My husband, Phil, noticed that The Book either had five stars or none at all; readers were entirely polarized about its value. No middle-ground opinions here: Some enthusiasts gushed on as though this guide were the Holy Grail that solved all of their parenting dilemmas, while other, more disillusioned, readers accused the authors of being clueless at best or abusive at worst.

On the appointed day, we followed The Book's advice by clearing our schedules, putting our two-and-a-half-year-old daughter in underpants and a T-shirt, and teaching her stuffed animals how to use the potty. Yes, her stuffed animals. The Book had suggested this as a first step. So Phil cut up an old white sock and designed some very sleek underwear for Mouse and Monkey before giving them their own "potties" (colorful, small plastic cups). Jerusha had a delightful hour teaching them how to use the potty, pull up their pants afterward, and carefully wash their hands. Meanwhile, we plied her with juice and promised her many, many treats if she would just use the potty herself.

Around lunchtime, we were standing in the kitchen when urine began trickling down Jerusha's legs, quickly forming a small puddle on the floor. In midbabble, our happy toddler looked down with distress at this stream of warm pee-pee and started to cry. As The Book had instructed, we hurried her to the toilet and had her finish the job there, following the whole process of pulling up pants and washing hands. I looked to The Book for additional guidance, noting that it never even mentioned the act of wiping. In fact, it seemed to assume that all children were male. A seed of doubt crept into my mind. Didn't these esteemed physicians think of wiping? Did they do all of their testing on boys?

Looking back, the rest of that week is something of a fog. Unable to leave the house, we cheered and praised Jerusha's few successes and tried not to become despondent about her many accidents. We were so stressed out that we found ourselves devouring almost all of the M&Ms we'd bought to encourage her successful potty use. As the week wore on, I became increasingly critical of The Book and even found myself logging on to the Amazon Web site again to reexamine what those other parents had said. Yep, I could certainly sympathize with the mother who considered the method—which required the toddler to clean up all of "his" own messes—to be abusive. I could see in Jerusha's eyes that the poor kid really didn't yet understand what was happening to her body, that she was afraid, and that above all she wanted our approval.

Our friends told us to fight the good fight, to keep pushing. Their children, of course, had easily and quickly mastered the technique, with a little persuasion. And I could certainly see their point; what if Jerusha *were* the only kid in her college dorm who still needed Mom to change her diapers? Would she ever be potty trained if we gave up now? Were Depends as expensive as Pampers?

An ancient proverb says that after eight days, a puppy's eyes are opened. So were ours. After eight days, we trashed The Book. Well, that's not quite true; we are simply incapable of actually throwing books away. But we did log on to Amazon.com to register our two cents' worth. And I had a heart-to-heart with Jerusha.

"Do you want to wear a diaper today, instead of using the potty, sweetheart?" I asked.

"Yeah," she said, obviously relieved, and looking much happier. Our sunny girl had returned. And in that moment, I loved her with such a gentle tenderness and a fierce protectiveness that my eyes spilled over with tears. I wanted so much for her to feel contented and secure. That was the end of potty training.

It was also the end of my letting the so-called experts call the shots where my child is concerned. As a parent, I know that there will be times when I am forced to make tough decisions about what is best for Jerusha's welfare, and I hope that I'm open to many points of view. However, I think the best advice I've received to date came from my own mom, who, when called upon at our baby shower to contribute a few words of advice to the expectant parents, simply said, "Follow your hearts." It's advice I intend to heed.

As a postscript, Jerusha's stuffed animals are all now completely potty-trained, from the pioneering mavericks, Mouse and Monkey, to Turtle and Ojo the bear. Jerusha faithfully rehearses the entire potty routine with them. "I wipe Ojo's dirty butt," she'll say, gleefully employing six or seven diaper wipes for the purpose. I suppose I should thank the authors of The Book, because in all the months since that terrible week last August, those animals have not had a single accident.

Jana Riess, the Religion Book Review Editor for *Publishers Weekly*, is the author of *The Spiritual Traveler: Boston and New England*.

⊷

I know what it is that is so scary about those little people be-tween the ages of one and four—they are raw and uncensored examples of our human nature. They are the urges, frustrations, desires, and fears that all of us feel, but they have absolutely no veneer of civilization to make them more palatable to their fellow human beings. It's as if your most egotistical friend mated with your worst date in high school and their baby shared DNA with Evel Knievel.

Maturity is really just a matter of learning clever ways to cover up the lively toddler in all of us. I still don't like to sit still in my chair, eat my vegetables, share my toys, or wait my turn to do absolutely anything; I'm just a lot better now at pretending all those things come naturally to me. Being around toddlers is too much like reading Lord of the Flies—*the more you know about them, the closer you feel to absolute anarchy.*

—Vicki Iovine

Too much is made of the Terrible Twos and not enough of the Metaphysical Fours. Around four, Casey began to look at the world with such a pure and unfettered intelligence I felt as if I were in a philosophy exam every night. The fourth year is a wonderful, metaphysical age, when he began to tackle the meaning of life completely free from any system of thought or the social conformity that sets in when they go to school. Along came the Big Questions, the ones about sex and death.

—Marni Jackson
Toronto, Canada

Kids notice things, like the patterns on the insides of flowers, for instance, all manner of those miraculous particulars so easily lost on potentially jaded grown-up eyes. Our kids insist on putting these little miracles in front of us, so that we're forced to reckon with them. Or perhaps they have an unselfconscious knack for coining Zen koans. My most recent favorite was Noah, my five-year-old's question: "Hey, Mom, what's the op-

posite of garlic?" My brain is still frozen from that one, but my heart is warm with reinvigorated wonder. Thanks, Noah.

—Sharon Lebell
Woodacre, California

Home Alone

By Lori Borgman

There's a world of difference between quiet and empty. Quiet is the blissful sound of children taking afternoon naps—it's an audible, treasured peace. Empty is the thumping of a solitary heartbeat and the echo of one lone voice in a house.

For the first time in eleven years, our house feels empty. Our "baby" has entered first grade. All three kids are gone all day now, until 2:42 P.M. to be precise. It's just me. Home alone.

I'm no longer the mother of a kindergarten student, preschool kid, or toddler. Cookie Monster and Mr. Rogers won't be stopping by on PBS. It's past time to take the safety plugs out of the electrical outlets and bid farewell to preschool carpools. There'll be no slathering shaving cream on the kitchen counter to create wild and wonderful art before 9 A.M. Raffi needn't serenade me anymore while I'm doing errands. But I can't give up the lullabye tape:

I like your eyes;
I like your nose;

I like your mouth,
Your ears, your hands, your toes.
I like your face
It's really you;
There's no one else exactly like you.

It seems like only yesterday that melody was playing during middle-of-the-night feedings. I can still smell the sweet scent of their newborn skin and see the variation of color in each baby's eyes. Time stands still for mommas with babes in their arms.

Then you blink twice, and your little people have mastered rolling over and sitting up. They've kicked off their booties and slid into laceless high-tops overnight. The cute little T-shirts branded "I love Mom" have vanished—replaced by tank tops with cocky, lime-green stegosaurus riding on a surfboard and brandishing an electric guitar. Before you can say "immunization records," they've swapped their training pants for Batman and Barbie lunch boxes and headed off to school.

BRR-UM! they're gone. Just like the big yellow school bus in the Little Golden Books *Car and Trucks,* they disappear with a roar. I thought this day would never come.

For more than a decade, the boundaries of my life have largely been this house and a three-mile radius that includes the grocery store, the pediatrician, and the preschool. We've had fun days of playing, silliness, exploring, and wonderment. We've also had days where the fur flew as we've fought like tomcats staking out territory. There have been days I wondered about the freedoms that were outside my front door. And at times I yearned for the door to open— just a crack.

The first breeze seemed to dry the spit-up trailing down my shoulder and soothe the frustrations of communicating with preverbal creatures. Gradually the door opened farther with each milestone the children passed: eating table food, potty training, making their own beds, riding their bikes without training wheels.

Suddenly the door was ajar far enough they could all shove past me to catch the school bus. Mysteriously, the long list of very important and urgent grown-up projects I was panting to get at seems insignificant, if not downright dull.

Maybe it's because I'm savoring the smaller freedoms first. If I want to eat M&Ms and rattle the bag, I can. If I want to grocery shop without someone running the cart over the back of my heels, I can. If I want to leisurely stroll through the crystal department of a department store, I can.

But if I want to snatch those kids back to recapture a few more days of finger painting and building forts with the dining room chairs, I can't. They're past all that now. The door's swung open wide to another season of life.

And if I've said it once, I've said it a million times, "Will someone please shut the door!" It feels a tad chilly in this empty house.

Lori Borgman is a nationally syndicated columnist on parenting and family life, and is the author of *I Was a Better Mother Before I Had Kids*.

Up in heaven a child was ready to be born. The child asked God, "I know you are sending me to earth tomorrow, but how can I survive there? I am so small and helpless."

God replied, "I have chosen a special angel for you there. She will love you and take care of you."

"Here in heaven, Lord, I don't do anything but sing and smile. What will I do on Earth? I won't know how to sing the songs down there."

"Your angel will sing for you," God replied, "and she'll teach you how to sing, too. And you'll learn to laugh as well as smile. Your angel and I will take care of that."

"But how will I understand what people say to me? I don't know a single word of the language they speak!"

"Your angel will say the sweetest things you will ever hear, and she will teach you, word by word, how to speak the language."

"And when I want to talk to You . . . ?"

"Your angel will gently place your little hands together and teach you how. That's the simplest language of all. It's called prayer."

"Who will protect me there, God?"

"Your angel is soft and gentle, but if something threatens you, there is no stronger force on Earth than the power she'll use to defend you."

"I'll be sad not getting to see You anymore."

"I will always be next to you, even though you can't see Me. And your angel will teach you the way to come back to Me if you stray."

Then it was time to go. Excited voices could be heard from Earth, anticipating the child's arrival. In a hurry, the babe asked softly, "Oh, God, if I must go now, please tell me my angel's name!"

And God replied, "You will call your angel . . . Mom."

—Author Unknown

God could not be everywhere and therefore He made mothers.

—Jewish proverb

SEVEN

Motherhood, the Great Refiner

We start our mothering careers as rather ordinary-looking clay pots with varied shapes and curves—and march directly into the refiner's fire. The fire, however, is not a onetime process but an ongoing one. Every experience that helps us to be a little more compassionate, a little more patient, a little more understanding, is a burst of fire that refines us and leaves us a little more purified. The more we filter, strain, and purge through the experience of our lives, the more refined we become.

—Linda Eyre
Salt Lake City, Utah

I don't remember who said this, but there really are places in the heart you don't even know exist until you love a child.

—Anne Lamott

I always wanted children, but not until they were actually part of my life did I realize that I could love that fiercely, or get that angry.

—Cokie Roberts

We have children because mothering is good for the soul. Having kids won't make us rich. It won't make our lives more tranquil. We do it because it's good for the soul.

—Ariel Gore
Oakland, California

Motherhood is not for the fainthearted. Used frogs, skinned knees, and the insults of teenage girls are not meant for the wimpy.

—Danielle Steel

Two Daughters and Six Days of the Flu

By Kate Young Caley

We are all damp with fever. It is only day six of this particular bout with the flu but it feels endless. We've lain, entangled on the couch, sick mother and two sick daughters forever it seems—a box of tissues and a row of dirty juice glasses lined up on the windowsill behind us. We drift in and out of confused sleep and, when awake, stare out the huge picture window and wait to feel well again.

My oldest daughter, Elizabeth, who is seven, has the best seat on the couch. She is the sickest and not about to let me forget it. I have a pounding headache and don't have the energy to explain to her why it might be kinder to give me a little more room. But then I realize, it is not that she is purposely taking up the whole couch—she has grown so much she can't help it. She stretches her lean legs well across the length of the cushions and I am startled by how long she is. What happened? I want my little girl back: that daughter who took up just one cushion.

Small and compact. The way my youngest, Jennie, at three, still is. The one who cuddles her chubby toddlerness around me. I give her little neck a kiss and lean my head against the wall, close my eyes, and sigh.

But neither of the daughters wants me to rest. They want me to be at the ready for any need that might suddenly arise. Resting for the mom is not allowed.

"Don't close your eyes, Mama," the oldest daughter says.

I lift my eyelids and look evenly at her, trying to hide the exhausted irritation I feel. Someday she may sit crowded on a couch with her children, dizzy with flu, and need, desperately, to rest but her demanding daughter won't let her. Then she'll see what it's like.

But I don't say this. I resist revenge when I am able. The sins of the mothers visit upon the daughters often enough. Besides, her eyes, above the thumb she still sucks at times like this, are glassy and tired. She smiles charmingly and makes a sucking noise with her wet thumb and lips. A sound deeply familiar to me that reminds me, achingly, of the days of breast-feeding. I smile back at her.

"I want more apple juice," Jennie, the youngest, says, and I tell her I'll get it in a minute. "Can we get another baby?" she asks then, as if asking for apple juice and another baby are similar requests.

"Perhaps this is not the best day to discuss another baby," I say, and the older daughter smiles at me knowingly and pops her thumb out of her mouth to comment.

"If we have another baby, I don't want a boy," she says. "I hate Ninja Turtles."

I nod. This is not the first time I have heard this opinion.

"If we have a baby, I won't be little anymore," Jennie says.

"You won't?" I ask, and blow my nose. I am curious about the reasoning behind this.

"If we get a baby, I will be big like Lizzie."

For a moment, I picture her sturdy little body—all that lovely, toddler roundness—suddenly pulled lean and sharp the way it has happened with my oldest girl. I see two long sisters stretched on the couch, their legs overlapping.

Maybe we *should* try for another baby.

"I will still be the biggest, Jennie, even if we do get a baby," Elizabeth says. "You will never be as big as me."

I remind myself that when we are sick, it is hard to be generous of spirit. I blow my nose some more and try to think of what to say to intervene, but my mind is working slowly and I miss my chance.

"Lizzie hurt my feelings!" Jennie wails. It amazes me how quickly she is able to move to absolute hysterics. With me, and with most people I know, there is a crescendo of sorts: a movement from displeasure to tears to sobs. But not with this child.

"Jennie, honey," I say, and wipe her sopping face. "Don't worry about it. You are very big and wonderful." But

I know that this is not how she sees it. She may, in fact, never feel as big or as wonderful as her sister. I don't have a sister myself, but I have seen how this can go.

I reach for more tissue and wipe the smears from her face. I glare at the oldest as if to say "There isn't enough trouble today?" She pulls the blanket up under her chin, coughs dramatically, and closes her eyes.

Sometimes, when I don't know what else to do, I read them a book. This is one of those times. I pick one out from the basket on the floor and let the words take us where they do.

One-half of the book and they are asleep. A miracle. I look at them and breathe in the air, which is sour-sweet with fever and unbrushed teeth. I wipe sticky hair back from their foreheads. My youngest says something in her sleep. I don't catch it, but it sounds content.

She will be okay in life, that one. It is good she is the younger sister. She can take it. The older one has let her thumb drop from her mouth but her lips still hold a round, open shape, and it gives her a beatific look. She will be okay in life, too. She will adjust to having a sister and even come to love her. Intensely. She just doesn't know that yet.

Tomorrow is day four of our second round of antibiotics, and this batch might just be working: finally, no coughing. I blow my nose and notice that my head is getting clearer, too. I take a deep breath and let it out slowly. I make a plan. Tomorrow I will wash the sheets. They smell germy and damp. Fresh beds will make us feel better. I'll empty the wastebaskets brimmed with crumpled pink tissues and get Elizabeth to work on her school papers. Maybe we can all go for a walk. A walk is always good.

But not today. Today I have done all I can. I look at

them once more, close my eyes, and fall deeply, gratefully asleep.

Kate Young Caley is the author of *The House Where the Hardest Things Happened.* She is a speaker and workshop leader, and lives with her husband and their two daughters in Quincy, Massachusetts.

৵ৎ

Children keep you very humble and honest. They are souls for you to care for while you learn to grow and understand about love, life, and commitment yourself.

—Carole Durepos
Clovis, New Mexico

A mother is neither cocky nor proud, because she knows the school principal may call at any minute to report that her child had just driven a motorcycle through the gymnasium.

—Mary Kay Blakely

The Molding of a Mother

By Kass Dotterweich

The molding of our own unique and individual motherhood begins to take shape the minute we start thinking and dreaming about becoming a mother. For many of us, that moment is nothing more than a vague slice of memory dating back so many decades that we can only smile at the shadows where it first began.

Then, at some point, we get serious about our motherhood; we conceive, find our way through pregnancy, and deliver our child to a waiting world—and the molding of a mother is seriously under way. With time, we realize that we will be in this molding process for the rest of our lives.

As our children become adults, and we have the luxury of looking back over the years of their infancy, toddlerhood, childhood, and teenagehood, we get a glimpse of ourselves in the molding process. We can see those events that shaped both our finest qualities and our most wretched weaknesses. In that reflecting on our motherhood, we realize a quiet sense of wisdom at what we've learned about ourselves, other people, and the world in general. We also harbor a deep fear at what we know we still do not know—and perhaps do not want to learn.

Having watched my six children grieve through the process of their parents' divorce over twelve years ago, I am just now beginning to realize a molding of my own motherhood that will stroke and push, fold and stretch, knead and fashion me for the rest of my life: how the impact of the divorce still influences my children's primary relationships, even as adults.

When my youngest child, Thomas, at the age of eighteen, experienced his first major heartbreak, when he and his girlfriend of nearly a year "broke up," I felt the Potter's hand get rough with the clay of my heart. As I listened to my dear son sob with the pain of an aching heart, I so desperately wanted to take away the horrible "ouchy" and "make it all better." After all, that's what mothers do. Our child falls down and we pick him up, dab at the wound with a warm cloth, lovingly apply a healing bandage covered with figures of Big Bird, and coo things like "There, see . . . all better."

But the pain of a broken relationship is not so easily healed. Thomas came to me distraught, angry, surprised, confused, hurt—bleeding in ways that no warm cloth or bandage would begin to soothe. All I could do was hug him, hold his hand, encourage him to talk, and affirm his tears. In that wisdom molded within me through the years of being a mother, I knew, of course, that Thomas would be fine, that he would grieve and heal, and that there would be another love someday. I couldn't say that to Thomas in the moment. That wasn't what he needed. What he needed was to know that his mother could see and hear his pain—and I thought that's what I was doing.

Then Thomas helped me understand that, no, I was not really seeing and hearing his pain—that he was in agony from something deeper, older, and far more painful than a broken heart. In his own way, Thomas let me see the old wound from his parents' divorce that is still healing, that will take so many more years to heal—*his* wound, which will mold *me* as a mother in the years ahead.

Thomas's precious tears, twelve years later, fell heavily on the soil of my heart, creating a pressure that I could no longer ignore. In those hours, as I hurt for the two of us, I came to understand two important lessons about the molding of a mother, lessons I had yet to realize even after thirty-two years of motherhood: We do not choose the means by which we are molded—and, regardless of how much we may try to ignore it, delay it, or deny it, the molding will have its way.

Kass Dotterweich is a freelance writer and the mother of six children.

Interlude

Bobbie McCaughey and her septuplets. © Warren Taylor/Polaris Images

We've learned a lot about dependency—on others and on God. As a parent, as a human being, no one of us is intended to have to go it alone. We need to get past our pride, admit our needs, and depend on God to show His love and care for us—often through the people He's placed around us.

We're learning to be more open with others. By making ourselves more vulnerable, we open ourselves to relationship opportunities we would otherwise never have had.

Kenny and I have learned to value our relationship, our marriage, and what time we have together. The bits and pieces of time we are able to share together mean more to us now than they ever did.

We're constantly learning what we only thought we knew before—that parenting requires very real sacrifice—but that the rewards far exceed the demands. We're learning to enjoy our kids even as we sometimes struggle to meet their constant needs. We have experienced the truth of what I told Peggy Wehmeyer when she asked how we thought we could possibly meet all the emotional requirements of eight children. When God created the miracle of love, He gave it an amazing characteristic our human minds can't truly fathom. The love God created, the love He shares with us and wants us to share with others, is infinitely expandable. Love grows to fit the need.

We loved Mikayla with all our hearts when she was our only child; there was no more love to give her. But when our seven babies were born, God expanded the love in our hearts so that we could love each one of them just as much. That amazing love, God's love, originating with Him and shared with us to share with others, is the greatest miracle of all. And we're still learning and seeing what that means in our lives.

—Bobbi McCaughey,
mother of septuplets

Sometime I have to wonder: Who else could do this but God? We are so happy and grateful.

—Nkem Chukwu,
mother of septuplets

EIGHT

Teaching a Little, Learning a Lot

The shocks and goose bumps and passion of raising sons often caused in me that aching, delirious sensation Einstein once described as "the deep shudder of the soul in enchantment." For Einstein, this ache was relieved with tears when he heard the sweet swell of violins echoing through velveted symphony halls. For me, those tears often flowed in less elegant settings—frequently in emergency rooms, when the doctor finally emerged from behind the white curtain where one of my sons lay unconscious and announced, "He's going to be all right." I could

be wearing a ratty sweatshirt splattered with blood when that quivering shudder came, but in that moment I understood what love—maybe even redemption—felt like. . . . However unconsciously by now, motherhood informs every thought I have, influencing everything I do. More than any other part of my life, being a mother taught me what it means to be human.

—Mary Kay Blakely

I know why families were created, with all their imperfections. They humanize you. They are made to make you forget yourself occasionally, so that the beautiful balance of life is not destroyed.

—Anaïs Nin

Sometimes Hugh and I feel that if we have done anything right with our children it has been an accident and a miracle; often we realize, in retrospect, that the things we thought were best weren't really very good at all. Perhaps our children have taught themselves more on our mistakes than on our goodwill. But we still have the courage to make decisions, to say yes, here; no, there.

—Madeleine L'Engle

The "good mother" is continually reinvented.

—Shari Thurer
Boston, Massachusetts

Unexpectations

By Marisa Novak

*M*y doctor guesses the flu. My husband hopes it's a false alarm. I know it is real.

I know he is coming. It's just two days after Christmas and our visiting family has gone home. We are still recovering from the hustle of the holiday and try to relax. Instead I continue to rock back and forth alone in our dark bedroom watching the snowfall cling to tree branches outside. As I move, my body tightens and my breath shortens. An hour later, the snow can no longer distract me from tonight's fate. At six months' pregnant, I am going into labor.

Marisa Novak with sons Duncan and Connor.

Paul tries to convince me that it's Braxton-Hicks as we enter the hospital, but I can't hear him through my heavy breathing and uncontrollable sobbing. A faceless nurse just starting her shift sees us panicking and guides us into the unfamiliar corridors of the labor and delivery ward as if she knew that we've only lived in Naperville for a year and our hospital tour was scheduled for next month.

Between pain and screaming I try to convince the strangers hustling around me that it is too early. In their professional tone they urge me to focus and stay calm. I instead order the doctors and nurses to leave the baby inside; after all, he is only twenty-five weeks by rough calculation. I am the mother. It is my choice. But my body commands otherwise and quickly delivers a two-pound-eight-ounce baby boy. Baby Novak took less than twenty minutes to arrive.

By 11:20 P.M. my husband collapses on the couch next to my hospital bed and freezes in disbelief. The medical staff filters out of the stark operating room taking our unnamed son.

There is no baby for us to cradle. There is no ceremonious welcome for him. Instead, we are left alone to recover. Paul and I don't speak to each other again for three days.

Then I start to ask the unanswerable: What happened? What now? Why? I wasn't high risk. I ate well. I exercised. I took care of myself. But six months and here he is . . . Baby Novak.

We wait for the test results to map out his future, our family's future. With a special needs child we will have to educate two-year-old Connor, the extended family, and ourselves. We have financial and health insurance issues to consider for long-term care. What about Connor and the burden he may carry if Baby Novak is handicapped? How could I let this happen?

Seventy-two hours later Dr. Covert personally unfolds the miracle to me as Paul phones the insurance company in the lobby. The test results showed no bleeding on the brain . . . I wept a prayer of thanks . . . No severe long-term effects are expected, although we still have roughly three months of development and high-risk factors to overcome.

Paul reenters to find me in a ball. He immediately expects the worst and sits down, covering his face with shaking hands. I relieve him by explaining that I am crying tears of joy. We hug and cry together. Finally we begin talking again. Our first conversation since the birth. We proudly name our son Duncan.

As hours and days pass, we carve a role for ourselves as parents of a preemie. It's the one pregnancy story that is hardly told. You sit and stare into an isolette with your child strapped to machines, a feeding tube, breathing tube, and IV. Not knowing what each minute brings you keep vigil with heavy eyelids.

We decorate Duncan's isolette with family pictures and buy CDs of classical, jazz, and "new-wave" music to play for him. A cross, other religious symbols, and messages grace his new artificial womb as a reminder of our unfailing faith.

The nurses and doctors are his main caregivers now, and I begin to feel helpless and depressed. Sometimes even my touch, his mother's own hold, can cause him to stop breathing or his heart to stop pumping. I am ripped apart knowing that my life-giving love is destructive. But the nurses, sensing my guilt, save me by telling me not to question my worth and my presence. After hours of practicing how to embrace his frail body, how to recline with him between my breasts, I finally feel a connection and a glimmer of hope. My son knew I was there. With his ears upon my bare chest he captures a heartbeat and indulges himself in my scent with every short breath. We become one again as if I am still nurturing him as nature intended. It is bliss.

Months pass and Duncan thrives. We leave the hospital near his due date in March as better parents. We have drawn strength from family and faith. My marriage survives a deep depression and is growing more passionate with each passing day. And as a mother of a preemie, I am more accepting, more cognizant of the fragility of life, and even more convinced that motherhood is life's noblest quest.

Marisa Novak is the mother of two boys and lives in Naperville, Illinois.

❧

Mothering has taught me more about letting go, being in the moment, unconditional love, grace, wisdom, joy, patience, and sacrifice than yoga, Buddhist meditation, Sufi dancing, Christian prayer, and psychotherapy combined.
—Elizabeth Lesser
Rhinebeck, New York

Through our children we . . . have a kind of spiritual reprieve.
—Edith F. Hunter

Kids teach you things about yourself you couldn't learn on your own—lessons about patience and selflessness, love and letting go. In my life, I'd gone way past control freak all the way to control monster. But my children have taught me to let things

Maria Shriver holding her daughter
Katherine Schwarzenegger in 1991.
© Brina Quigley/Timepix

*roll off my back, to be flexible, to accept them even when they
don't think/act/feel exactly as I do.*

—Maria Shriver

Unlearning Harvard

By Martha Beck

$\mathcal{I}$t is a frightening thing to love someone you know the
world rejects. It makes you so terribly vulnerable. You know
you will be hurt by every slight, every prejudice, every pain
that will befall your beloved throughout his life. In the wee

small hours, as I rocked and nursed and sang to my wee small boy, I couldn't help but worry. Will Rogers once said that he knew worrying was effective, because almost nothing he worried about ever happened. That's a cute statement, and I'm glad Will's life worked this way. But mine hasn't—at least not where Adam is concerned. Almost everything I worried about during the nights after his birth, almost every difficult thing I feared would come my way as a result of being his mother, has actually happened.

Thank God.

What my fears all boiled down to, as I sat with my tiny orange son in the days after his birth, was an underlying terror that he would destroy my own facade, the flawlessness and invulnerability I projected onto the big screen, the Great and Terrible Martha of Oz. You see, I knew all along that there wasn't one label people might apply to Adam—stupid, ugly, strange, clumsy, slow, inept—that could not, at one time or another, be justifiably applied to me. I had spent my life running from this catastrophe, and like so many other things, it caught up with me while I was expecting Adam.

In this regard, as in so many others, my worst fears have come to pass. But as they do, I am learning that there is an even bigger secret, a secret I had been keeping from myself. It has been hard for me to grasp, but gradually, painfully, with the slow, small steps of a retarded child, I am coming to understand it. This has been the second phase of my education, the one that followed all those years of school. In it, I have had to unlearn virtually everything Harvard taught me about what is precious and what is garbage. I have discovered that many of the things I thought were priceless are as cheap as costume jewelry and much of what

I labeled worthless was, all the time, filled with the kind of beauty that directly nourishes my soul.

Now I think that the vast majority of us "normal" people spend our lives trashing our treasures and treasuring our trash. We bustle around trying to create the impression that we are hip, imperturbable, omniscient, in perfect control, when in fact we are awkward and scared and bewildered. The irony is that we do this to be loved, all the time remaining terrified of anyone who seems to be as perfect as we wish to be. We go around like Queen Elizabeth, bless her heart, clutching our dowdy little accessories, avoiding the slightest hint of impropriety, never showing our real feelings or touching anyone else except through glove leather. But we were dazed and confused when the openly depressed, bulimic, adulterous, rejected Princess Di was the one people really adored.

Living with Adam, loving Adam, has taught me a lot about truth. He has taught me to look at things in themselves, not at the value a brutal and often senseless world assigns to them. As Adam's mother I have been able to see quite clearly that he is no less beautiful for being called ugly, no less wise for appearing dull, no less precious for being seen as worthless. And neither am I. Neither are you. Neither is any of us.

Of course, I haven't gone far enough in my reeducation to have left my early training completely behind me. The stupidity, the shortsightedness, the narrowness of this shadow world still hurt me from time to time. It hurt me when, three days after his birth, I carried Adam in his little front-pack to finish up my year at Harvard, and not one student or faculty member commented on the fact that he'd been born. They wouldn't even look at him. Those who had to speak to me kept their eyes resolutely fixed on my face, as though looking down a few inches at Adam's would pull them tumbling into some inescapable abyss.

That was only the beginning. Just as I feared, Adam and I have experienced mockery and judgment and exclusion, and they have all been painful. It hurts every time people look at Adam and see only the deformity of their own perceptions, instead of the beauty before their eyes. But more and more, I feel this pain not for my son but for the people who are too blind to see him. The lessons I have learned from Adam have hurt more than just about anything else I ever felt in my life. And it's been worth it, a thousand times over.

Martha Beck is the author of the national best-seller, *Expecting Adam,* and is the mother of three children.

❧

You will see the divinity in every creature.
—Bhagavad Gita

Every child comes with the message that God is not yet discouraged of man.
—Rabindranath Tagore

A baby is God's opinion that the world should go on.
—Carl Sandburg

Losing Robin

By Barbara Bush

Jeb was just a few weeks old when Robin woke up one morning and said, "I don't know what to do this morning. I may go out and lie on the grass and watch the cars go by, or I might just stay in bed." I didn't think that sounded like a normal three-year-old and decided she must have what my mother called "spring fever." I took her to our excellent pediatrician, Dr. Dorothy Wyvell. She examined Robin, took some blood, and told me she would call me after the test results were in. She suggested I might want to come back without Robin, but with George. That sounded rather ominous to me, but I wasn't too worried. Certainly Robin had no energy, but nothing seemed seriously wrong.

Dr. Wyvell called, and George met me at her office in the late afternoon. Dorothy was not one to pull any punches. She told us Robin had leukemia. Neither of us had ever heard of it, and George asked her what the next step was; how did we cure her? She talked to us a little about red and white blood cells and told us as gently as possible that there was no cure. Her advice was to tell no one, go home, forget that Robin was sick, make her as comfortable as we could, love her—and let her gently slip away. She said this would happen very quickly, in several weeks. We talked a little more, and George asked her if she would talk to his uncle, Dr. John Walker, at Memorial Sloan-Kettering Hospital in New York City. She readily agreed. Uncle John also thought Robin had little chance to live, but he thought we should by all means treat her and try to extend her life, just in case of a breakthrough.

I drove home, and George had to return to the office for just a minute. On the way, he stopped at Liz and Tom Fowler's house and asked Liz please to come over to be with me. By that evening our living room was filled with close friends, all offering to help. I remember being so surrounded by love that I did not really believe what the doctor had told us was true. She just had to be wrong. But either way, we knew we had to do everything we could to save our beautiful child.

Leukemia was not a well-known disease. Many people thought it was catching and did not let their children get near Robin. In those days, cancer in general was only whispered about, and some people just couldn't cope with a dying child. It was not an easy time for our friends or us.

I made up my mind that there would be no tears around Robin, so I asked people who cried to step out of her room. I didn't want to scare our little girl. Poor George had the most dreadful time and could hardly stand to see her get a blood transfusion. He would say that he had to go to the men's room. We used to laugh and wonder if Robin thought he had the weakest bladder in the world. Not true. He just had the most tender heart.

Rightly or wrongly, we did not tell six-year-old Georgie that his sister was dying. We hated that, but we felt it would have been too big a burden for such a little fellow. On the other hand, there could be no more roughhousing since leukemia patients easily hemorrhage, so we had to keep a close watch on them when they were together.

One day, back in New York, George's father asked me

to go with him to the graveyard in Greenwich. He wanted me to see where he would be buried. The lot he picked was lovely, on a nice hillside with trees. He was such a dear man, and he picked out a modest headstone that said BUSH— about three feet tall and four feet wide. On one side of the headstone was a freshly planted lilac bush; on the other side, a dogwood tree. It was a sunny, bright day, and Dad pointed out some enormous mausoleum-type buildings or large headstones. Then he said, "I knew old so-and-so. He certainly thought highly of himself, didn't he, Bar?" That darling man bought that lot so Robin would have a place to rest.

Eventually the medicine that was controlling the leukemia caused other terrible problems. We called George, and by the time he got there after flying all night, our baby was in a coma. Her death was very peaceful. One minute she was there, and the next she was gone. I truly felt her soul go out of that beautiful little body. For one last time I combed her hair, and we held our precious little girl. I never felt the presence of God more strongly than at that moment.

George and I love and value every person more because of Robin. She lives on in our hearts, memories, actions, and through the Bright Star Foundation. I don't cry over her anymore. She is a happy, bright part of our lives.

Barbara Bush is former first lady of the United States, the mother of five children, and the grandmother of fourteen grandchildren.

Carlos Broxton in 1982.

February 28, 1982, will stay on my mind for the rest of my life. I relied on my faith and on prayer in accepting the death of my son.

—Fredericka Broxton
Annapolis, Maryland

I have known the pain of murder and have grieved with many other parents of murdered children. Buoyed by the grace of God, I found my answer. It is ever to work for and celebrate life.

—Antoinette Bosco
Brookfield, Connecticut

The Poyer clan.

Boom!

By Marie Poyer

I have Boomers. Baby Boomers.
Lots of them. Fourteen. That's lots.
They came in two varieties. Boys and girls. Seven of each.
They came to live in my heart from 1947 to 1964. They
never left.

They came with tiny fingers tucked inside my hand, sticky
kisses plopped upon my cheeks, and eyes of brown
and eyes of blue that followed my every move.

The angels that sent them down equipped them with
skates and scooters and bikes and all the toes and
arms and legs to ride and pedal and scoot. And
laundry.

All but one. One little girl must have hidden behind a
cloud on the day the finishing touches were spread
around. She stayed a few short years and went Home
to open up some rooms for the rest of us at the B&B
in the Sky.

They came with hot dogs and cookies, diapers and
skinned knees, homework and carpools, chocolate and
Cheerios, socks that never match, footballs and
baseball bats and swim meets and proms. And
laundry.

There came a day when they gave their hearts away to that
cute boy from English Lit or that little redhead at 31
Flavors. There were bridal gowns and flowers, tuxes
and boutonnieres, new homes and cars and starry eyes
and dreams.

Now I have Boomettes. Baby Boomers' Babies.
Lots of them. Thirty-five. That's lots.
They came in two varieties too. Boys and girls.

They came mixed with Irish and Italian, Polish and
    German, Dutch and Latino, Jewish and Lebanese,
    French and Yugoslavian, Native American and
    Canadian.
And laundry.

One day I blinked and the Boomettes were Boomin'!
And the sticky kisses keep on coming and the eyes still
    follow me around and so many fingers, large and
    small, are tucked inside my heart.

So many years. So much love to give and take. So much
    laundry. So many socks that were impossible to
    match.

I love being a Mom.

Marie Poyer is the mother of thirteen children and grandmother
of thirty-five grandchildren. She lives in Encino, California.

NINE

One to Chaos

The first child got me shiny new, like a new pair of shoes, but he got the blisters, too. The second child got me worn, yes, but comfortable. I told the first child I would never go away, and I lied. I told the second child I would always come back, and spoke the truth. The second child had a mother who knew that the proper response to a crying baby was not to look up "Crying, causes of" in the index of Dr. Spock. As a matter of fact, he had a mother who was too busy to read child care books at all, and

*so was in no position to recognize whether his "developmental
milestones" were early/late/all/none of the above.*

—Anna Quindlen

*I think three kids is the hardest number, because you start play-
ing zone defense. After that, it's like my mom always said:
"Another kid, you just put on another potato."*

—Marie Osmond

*When Shayla was born, I didn't think I could love anyone or
anything as much as I loved her. But then, the same was true
with McKenna when she was born two years later.*

—Mary Lou Retton

Former Olympic gymnast Mary Lou Retton with infant daughter
Shayla. © Barbara Laing/Timepix

Sylvia Walter holds only-child Elizabeth.

My One and Only

By Sylvia Walter

It wasn't until my daughter was three and a half that I realized she was going to be an only child. I found out I liked it that way.

The advantages are many . . . like only having to coordinate one child's activities. I always felt sorry for other mothers who couldn't drop their kid off at, say, dancing lessons and go home. They had to go pick up or drop off another one somewhere completely different. And you only have one child to dress in the morning, just one to get ready to go. Compared to my friends with multiple children, my job was a breeze. I could devote all of my time to my daughter, taking her to all of her lessons, and giving her everything I could afford or thought she needed. I gave her all my love.

And now that she is on her own I don't have other kids to get through high school, college, or a wedding. When you have an only child, you are pretty much on your own as soon as she is grown up. You don't have that "empty nest" feeling. My husband and I had plenty of practice at being alone before she grew up—when she went to sleepovers and, of course, college. There was never that gap, that feeling that, all of a sudden, no one is around and you're standing in an empty house.

They say only children fare much better in the world, have more confidence, and are surer of themselves. I think that is true of my only child. She has those qualities.

On the other side of it, being the mother of an only child can be rough on the child. All your hopes and dreams rest on that one kid's shoulders. You don't have another kid to go to if that one doesn't do what you want. You don't have another one to be what you wanted the first to be.

We thought we could make our daughter any way we wanted, but soon learned we had an individual on our hands. We wanted her to be a lawyer; she, of course, did not. She would never do what we wanted. She always had to do it her way. We did, however, teach her to make her own decisions.

The other day while going through our family picture albums my elderly mother kept asking my daughter who this or that child was and my daughter pointed out that "They're all me, Grandma." That is life with an only child—we have fourteen picture albums and every picture in them is of her. She was always there, posing and saying "Take my picture." To this day almost every picture in our house has my daughter in it.

I do not regret having an only. I know we made the right decision. We had the perfect kid already and another couldn't compare.

Sylvia Walter lives in New Jersey with her husband of thirty-three years and is the proud mother of an only child.

❧

One is a very good number.

—Tracy Lose
Annapolis, Maryland

Yin and Yang

By Mary Lynn Hendrickson

We should have noticed the signs early on. First there were the ultrasounds: The shots of my son in the lower right corner of my abdomen showed him lying back and lazily contemplating the wave of his fingers in the amniotic fluid. My daughter, perched at the top left, was so busy somersaulting that we couldn't get a clear enough picture to tell if she was going to be a boy or a girl.

Then came those last nervous weeks of my pregnancy, when I was sent home with a little chart to mark off the movements of each baby in utero. Katie kept me awake with the well-placed kicks and head butts of a Brazilian soccer team. Mr. Slug, on the other hand, had me clinging white knuckled to the handset of a cordless phone, my

"Opposite Twins" James and Katie.

twitching fingers rehearsing the 9–1–1 sequence that would summon the paramedics.

Fast-forward the endless camcorder footage of their lives, and you see two very different babies bobbing side-by-side in their high chairs. Thinking scarcity, she would grab things—soggy Cheerios, teething rings, rugged rubber baby whatchamahoozits—from her brother. Thinking abundance, he would part with such things with only a moment of detached curiosity before moving on to something new.

Fast forward again: They are toddlers at a Christmas party, Katie near the center of a manic swirl of older kids, laughing and dancing and falling all over each other like roughhousing puppies. James wanders in from time to time to cheer them on and add his excited yelps to the din, but he passes much of the evening quietly raking the miniature sandbox of my friends' tabletop serenity garden. She can't get enough of these kids; he can't get far enough away.

The "Opposite Twins," we call them, a direct reference

to the twin piglets from a Richard Scarry video, a brother and sister who do a little ditty to demonstrate the concept of opposites to preschoolers. Or "Yin and Yang," as my husband likes to call them. Today they are kindergarteners, and like most little girls Katie grooves on pink, purple, and ponies. She likes to color and sing and read and spell—usually all at the same time. James loves Legos and *The Adventures of Captain Underpants,* a couple of passions he can indulge single-mindedly for hours at a time. She's a theatrical extrovert, like my husband's side of the family. People like her grow up to be one of the overwrought characters in a Woody Allen movie. He's an observant introvert, like the people from my own family tree. I'm descended from the kind of wordless Norwegian farmers who could get excited watching grass grow.

She goes for meat, he loves fruits and vegetables—a Jack Spratt couple if ever there was one. He could wear his shoes on the wrong feet all day and never notice; she needs to wear even the thinnest socks inside out so that the seams don't bother her. As a baby, she liked the traditional pacifier with the ring and straight nipple. He fancied the curved orthodontic tip that was glued into a large colorful button. As infants, their grandmothers each gave them a set of blankets to cuddle with; the two "Grandma Peggy" blankets were homemade and crocheted while the pair of "Grandma Mary" blankets were an elegant weave from a top millinery. God forbid they should like the same things: And so James quickly inherited both Grandma Mary blankies and Katie the set from Grandma Peggy.

Oh, and as if anybody really needed to ask: She uses her left hand and he uses his right.

"You're so lucky," complete strangers would say to us as

we used to wheel their double stroller through the park. "You have one of each, a boy and a girl—a complete set." Yes, a set. What would night be without the day after all, or salt without pepper? Push without pull, yin without yang?

As opposite as they are, my kids can be each other's best friend or worst enemy. They are like magnets that when held one way, smack together with all the speed and force of nature—magnets that, when held differently, repel each other with powerful force.

When my twins are on the same page—swirling around the house in Harry Potter spectacles and on anything they can turn into a broomstick—they are the picture of twosome togetherness, their differences forming the epoxy glue that bonds them. At such times they are the picture of cavorting complementarity—like Abbott and Costello, Lucy and Desi, Laverne and Shirley, Mutt and Jeff, Ernie and Bert. For all his inward imagination, he dances to the music of a different drummer; for all her outward energy, she simply loves to dance. And when they find a way to do it together, boy, do they ever have a blast.

But, oh, let there be trouble in River City and the beautiful music they make together turns into a symphony of sour notes. "James won't let me play with him," wails my daughter when my introverted son has had too much togetherness and proclaims that he and his LEGOs are suddenly on sabbatical. "Katie will only let me have one can of white Play-Doh," he whines pitifully, as my humming daughter cranks out multicolored creations by the dozen. More than once, there were even sightings of "my evil twin" in their preschool room—my daughter mysteriously spilling my son's milk from afar, or so he claimed—so that they were gently separated into different rooms the following year, James thriving under the patient, watchful eye of soft-spoken Mrs. C. and Katie glorying in the constant flow of worksheets and craft projects cooked up by Mrs. D.

Having twins, I suppose, can seem exotic and out of the ordinary. But to my husband and me, it's as normal as a blue sky. It's all we know. And frankly, our kids' many differences usually blind us to the fact that they are even twins at all. It's not until we sit back and really think about it, out of detachment or exhaustion, that we are amazed by our situation at all—especially how lucky we are that they were born so healthy, how incredible it is that he and I survived all the feedings and all the colic and all the frustrations of potty training. (Would you believe that my kids even favored different kinds of potty chairs?)

For us, having two kids the same age seems utterly natural—the real reason for tandem bikes and teeter totters, why a mom has two legs for a pair of timid toddlers to cling to, why a dad has a hand for each preschooler to hold, why there is one parent each for them to run to with scraped knees and ladybugs in a jar. But the very best thing about our "complete set": We learned, early on, that we can say "You are my favorite girl in the whole wide world" and "You are my favorite little boy in the universe" and have it be absolutely true, absolutely guilt-free, without slighting the other. We just couldn't say both of those things if we happened to have three children instead of our two. And for that we are truly grateful.

Mary Lynn Hendrickson works from her home in Stoughton, Wisconsin, where she gets paid to direct the Associated Church Press and has the privilege of parenting six-year-old Katie and James Gagen, her only children with husband John Gagen.

❦

When the phone is ringing, and the infant is fussing, and the toddler is whining about a Luke Skywalker action figure, and the seven-year-old can't find his shoes and is about to miss the school bus, and you turn on the computer and a little picture of a bomb appears with a message that reads, "Sorry, a system error has occurred," and the kettle is whistling, and the cat is hungry, and there is spit-up on your briefcase (the dark-brown leather one that appeared last Christmas and that you never wrote a thank-you note for but now it's too late because you can't remember who sent it), and you have to pee, and your lover is hogging the bathroom, and you get an e-mail message from a friend who is convinced that "the end is nigh," and you remember suddenly that your mother is coming for dinner and you had promised to make the chicken mole from the Frida Kahlo cookbook and you can't even begin to imagine where the cookbook is, and the infant is still fussing, and you step on the Luke Skywalker action figure and sprain your ankle, it's all right not to get frantic. Take a seat. Take a breath. And let yourself laugh. This is how it is meant to be sometimes.

—Ariel Gore

Oakland, California

I've learned to eat dinner in less than ten minutes, go to bed by 10 P.M., and take a shower in five minutes flat. I've also learned that my "to do" list for Monday may take me to Friday or the following Monday to complete.

—Clare Collins-Panzino

Frederick, Maryland

I wake up, figure out what we should defrost for dinner, and do all this running around.

—Debra Winger

The Three-Kid Digression

By Barbara Johnson

$\mathcal{B}$ecoming a parent changes everything, but parenthood itself also changes with each baby.

For example, consider your wardrobe. As soon as the pregnancy home test confirms that you're pregnant, you head for the mall—and come home wearing a maternity outfit. With the second baby, you squeeze into your regular clothes as long as possible. With the third baby, your maternity clothes *are* your regular clothes.

Then there's your preparation for labor and delivery. With the first baby, you attend weekly classes and faithfully practice your breathing. With the second baby, you try to keep breathing when you find your two-year-old teetering at the top of the basement stairs. With the third baby, you threaten to hold your breath indefinitely unless the doctor gives you an epidural in your second trimester.

Collecting the first baby's layette is always fun. You spend hours shopping for just the right curtains, blankets, and crib ruffle and carefully prewash the tiny little gown and booties with Woolite. For the second baby, you adjust the curtains and ruffles so the projectile-vomiting stains don't show and bleach everything else in hot water to disinfect it. With the third child, you move to Florida so the baby needs no clothes at all—just disposable diapers.

A new baby can cause overwhelming fatigue, so parents adapt different stress-coping strategies with each child. For instance, with the first baby, you worry so much about the baby's cries that you never put the infant down—you wear her constantly in a baby carrier strapped to your chest. When the second baby cries, you pick him up only when his hysterics threaten to wake up your firstborn. With the third child, you teach your other two kids where to look for the pacifier and how to rewind the baby swing.

Parents' dealings with the baby-sitters also change. The first time you leave your baby with a sitter, you conduct a two-hour training session for the caregiver, then call home four times while you run to the post office. With the second baby, just before you walk out the door you remember to leave an emergency phone number—your neighbor's. With the third baby, you tell the sitter to call only if someone needs stitches, splints, or an ambulance.

Baby activities change, too. You take the first infant to baby swim classes, baby aerobics, and baby massage. You take your second baby to baby story hour so you can nap while the story is read. You take the third baby to the McDonald's drive-through.

You use your time differently as each child comes along. You spend hours each day staring adoringly at your precious first infant. With the second baby, you glance in her direction occasionally as you race to stop your toddler from dropping the cat down the laundry chute. With the third child, you train the dog to guard the baby from his siblings a few hours each day while you hide in the closet.

While I love to laugh now at such silly evolutions, I do remember that babies can be fabulous—and lots of fun. A baby is a small member of the family who can make the love stronger, the days shorter, the nights longer, and the bankroll smaller. When a baby is born, the home will be happier—even if the clothes are shabbier. The past is forgotten, and the future is worth living for. And when more babies come along, the work is multiplied, that's true; but so are the joy and the love.

Barbara Johnson is a popular conference speaker and best-selling author. She and her husband, Bill, founded Spatula Ministries, an organization designed to peel parents off the ceiling with a spatula of love.

With her own mom, Margaret Vetter, Agnes Gaughan and her brood enjoy an outing at Freedomland, a 1960s version of Disneyland in the Bronx.

Agnes Gaughan holds her first
great-grandchild, Liam Michael.

❧

*At eighty years old, I can say that the most rewarding experi-
ence of my life is being a mom. My husband and I were blessed
with six children, each one with his or her own disposition and
individuality. From babyhood, there was something new to
learn from them every day.*

*Life around our house was pretty routine. We didn't go
away on vacations, but when Dad got his two weeks off each
year, there were day trips to Rockaway and Jones Beach, Coney
Island and the Bronx Zoo. We had a big yard, and I think
every boy on the block learned to play ball there with our two
sons. Then there were the Sweet 16 parties our four girls had in
our living room.*

*At Christmastime it was the writing of Santa Claus let-
ters weeks before and then putting up the big Christmas tree*

and decorating it. *There were happy and prideful times—First Communions, Confirmations, and weddings. There were also worrisome and sleepless nights during childhood sicknesses. But for every sleepless night there were a thousand moments of joy.*

Now with nineteen grandchildren and last month holding my first great-grandchild in my arms, I'd say I'm a very lucky and blessed mom.

—Agnes Gaughan
Bronx, New York

As a mother of eleven children, you have to be organized or else the inmates take over the asylum.

—Mary Clarke
Annapolis, Maryland

Interlude ❧

I am so grateful for having you for my mother—a woman of such fine spirit and unlimited devotion. You have been my inspiration, always, and whatever I am or become, the credit for all that is good will be yours.
—Lyndon Johnson
(to his mother)

From my mother, I learned the value of prayer, how to have dreams and believe I could make them come true.
—Ronald Reagan

All that I am or hope to be I owe to my angel mother. I remember my mother's prayers and they have always followed me. They have clung to me all my life.
—Abraham Lincoln

I remember how I clung to her till I was a great big fellow, but love of the best in womanhood came to me and entered my heart through those apron strings.
—Woodrow Wilson

All I am I owe to my mother . . . I attribute all my success in life to the moral, intellectual, and physical education I received from her.
—George Washington

TEN

Boy Oh Boy!

Boys are the best investments in the world. They pay the biggest dividends.

—Ida Eisenhower

Having had kids who represent each gender, I've noticed some unique characteristics. While both have healthy, active imagi-

nations, each goes about fulfilling that potential in decisively opposite ways. One hot summer day, the neighborhood kids, ages seven, eight, and nine, were all swimming in our pool. I observed that the little girls would swim more often in the shallow end. They were pretending they were otters. There was a mommy otter and two sister otters. The mommy otter was teaching her children how to swim on their backs with clams on their chests. Meanwhile the boys were seeing how far into the middle of the pool they could jump. I heard an inventive Billy exclaim, "I know, I'll fart!" Apparently he thought his gas would propel him farther into the pool.

—Marilyn Kentz

Los Angeles, California

If I've taught Ryan and Darren something about women and justice, my jock sons have taught me something about being a sport. In our ongoing discussions of gender politics, I've looked at the issues as urgently as ever, but through the lens of love and hope rather than anger and despair. By encouraging their greater compassion and maturity, I have grown and changed myself. Raising boys has made me a more generous woman than I really am. Undoubtedly, there are other routes to learning the wishes and dreams of the presumably opposite sex, but I know of none more direct, or more highly motivating, than being the mother of sons.

—Mary Kay Blakely

My Three Sons

By Denise Roy

$\mathcal{I}$ knew by the time I was ready to deliver my third child that it would be a boy. My identity was already shaped as the mother of sons.

So I was not surprised when, seventeen years ago, I brought Matthew Thomas home from the hospital to meet his brothers: Benjamin James, who was then four years old, and David Christopher, who was two years old. For the next two decades, these three boys would fill the house with laughter and noise, roughhousing and playfulness.

In raising my sons, I tried my best not to fall into gender stereotyping. I bought them stuffed animals and dolls

Denise Roy and family.

when they were little, and a toy stove for them to cook on. I outlawed guns. I talked to them about inclusive language, and read books that had girls as well as boys as heroes.

Little good that did. The boys attacked their stuffed animals with large plastic dinosaurs. They chewed American cheese slices into pistols and flapped them menacingly at one another. After cooking on their stove, they turned it into a fort. And they wrestled constantly, spending hours entwined with one another, rolling down the hall like giant tumbleweeds.

Our house still bears the traces of the whirlwind that passed through during these years. A couch with only three legs, one broken off during a wrestling match, is now supported on one side with bricks. A hole in the window screen from a hand that was pushed through it continues to let mosquitoes in on summer nights. Trophies from a gazillion sporting events fill bedrooms and boxes.

Even now, when they are six feet tall, my sons' constant energy and relentless activity never cease to amaze me—and cause me to be forever warning, "Watch out, someone will get hurt."

Over the years, there have been the normal day-to-day arguments and skirmishes, but overall the boys have gotten along pretty well. I remember taking them to a park many years ago, shortly after their father and I had separated. We had a joint custody arrangement, and the boys traveled together between two households. I knew they would need each other for support in the years to come. As I watched them spin on the merry-go-round, laughing with each other, I sent a prayer out into the universe: "May they always be friends with one another."

My prayers seemed to have been answered. When they

were little, I overheard one of their plans—to become fishermen and spend the rest of their lives together. I have photos of all three of them dressed as Superman for Halloween, of all three wearing karate outfits, of all three flexing their muscles for the camera.

They stick together like the Three Musketeers—"One for all and all for one." Take the time I went to the hospital to give birth to their baby sister six years ago. At the time, they were eleven, thirteen, and fifteen. They came to the hospital with their stepfather and me, and even though we had invited them to attend the birth, they decided to wait out in the hallway. Then David, my middle and most adventuresome son, announced, "I'm going in to watch. It's not every day you get the chance to see a birth."

The other two boys were not going to be left behind. Between contractions, I remember looking over and seeing the three of them sitting on the floor, trying to disguise their amazement at what they were witnessing. They held their baby sister within minutes of her birth and opened their circle to include their new sibling.

As I write this, my two oldest sons are home from college for spring break. The three are once again united, roughhousing and destroying what is left of our house, and once again I'm trying to understand the world they inhabit.

I'm enjoying what's left of their childhood, because I know their home isn't going to be with me forever. But they will always have each other with whom to wrestle, and play hoops, and attack with slices of American cheese chewed into pistols.

Denise Roy is the author of *My Monastery Is a Minivan* and lives in Santa Clara, California.

꧁

My mother taught me that my talent for singing was as much God's work as a beautiful sunset or a storm that left snow for children to play in.

—Michael Jackson

My mother never gave up on me. I messed up in school so much they were sending me home, but my mother sent me right back.

—Denzel Washington

My mother is my root, my foundation. She planted the seed that I base my life on, and that is the belief that the ability to achieve starts in your mind.

—Michael Jordan

A kiss from my mother made me a painter.

—Benjamin West

Baseball Mom

By Anna DiFranco

When I was eight months' pregnant, I attended my very first professional league baseball game. My mother-in-law and I chatted for most of the game, but not about baseball as I remember. My husband and his father were enjoying the bonds that united them in their love of the game.

The years rolled by and one darling, delightful son was joined by a second. In no time I was the mother of two lively boys who loved sports, especially baseball, and I really had no clue how this happened. My life was filled with gear, including gloves, bats, balls, cleats, uniforms, hats, helmets, leggings, and of course cups. Spring in our house wasn't about daffodils. It was about baseball.

Although it was a long time between my first and second attendance at a professional baseball game, I was busy learning the sport as I sat through many Little League games. However, the most important things I learned about baseball didn't happen at the field; they happened in the backyard. During the season I would stop cleaning up after dinner, stop folding the wash, stop grading my students' papers or doing my lesson plans when the screen door opened and my sons called me to the diamond of their childhood. I got to play every position in my long years of training, from fielder, to catcher, to pitcher. Some days I even got to bat. I'm not a very good athlete. They would tell me not to throw like a girl, which always got a laugh. Then they'd come over to the mound and give me my annual review, and I'd try my best to be one of the boys. I grew to love this game because they loved it, and they needed and included me in this love. I thought this way of life would last forever. How little I knew of time, because in time they grew up.

My sons never made it to the pro leagues as players, but in the intervening years we've had many wonderful days at the stadiums enjoying both major and minor league games. If you were to look at my backyard today you probably wouldn't see the worn spots, where every summer the diamond would come alive. But it is always there for me in sight, in sound, even in smell. In my heart, I'm still a base-ball mom.

Anna DiFranco is a baseball mom living in Matawan, New Jersey.

♨

I look out the window to see my two boys, five and three, in a rare moment of sibling harmony. They are squatting, side-by-side, engrossed by something at their feet. What wonder of nature has them so entranced? I wonder. Then my husband comes in from outside.

"They look so cute together," I comment. "For once they're not fighting."

"Yeah, they're looking for bugs so they can smash them with rocks," John reports matter-of-factly.

I know this isn't a PC thing to say, but as the mother of three boys, I'm constantly struck by how true the stereotypes are. Before I had children, I had the naive idea that they're largely a product of their environment. So, if we didn't allow violent TV and forbade toy guns, then our boys would be gentle, peace-loving individuals, happily engaged in building block towers or kicking a ball back and forth.

It turns out that you can—and my boys do—make a gun out of anything. Our house is overrun with action figures featuring characters from the shows I swore they'd never watch. (They must have found out about the Saturday morning episode of Power Rangers—*the highlight of their week—through osmosis, as we never pointed it out.)*

The gender thing doesn't just apply to TV, toys, and the propensity to get physical.

"I don't want the yellow cup," Jack asserts.

"What's wrong with yellow?" I asked with exasperation.

"That's a Barbie color."

So there are no ballet recitals in my future, and chances are they're not going to be interested in some of my favorite childhood books, such as A Little Princess. Still, they do have their sweet side. If I forget to kiss my three-year-old good-bye, my sitter says Matthew can be inconsolable for hours. And Jack, who's five, never fails to compliment me on a new pair of shoes. At nine months, Christopher is too young to know about the merits of pink versus blue or Powerpuff Girls versus Power Rangers. That will come soon enough.

—Kate Kelly
Pelham, New York

He is part alien, part boy, this son of mine. He crawls around the family room in cumbersome, awkward movements, unlike the small, graceful techniques of the little girls I see at the mall.

David enjoying a first few jumps.

At six months of age, he has mastered the remote control, acquired his own tool set from the untouchables hiding in the childproofed cabinets, and has already dismantled and "reassembled" all of the electronics in our home. Although he can't yet talk, I know that he will never, ever ask for directions. He is my little man, helping me to better understand and appreciate the common traits and fascinating quirks belonging to the opposite sex who inhabit the planet of Mars.

—Therese J. Borchard

My hope for my sons is that they grow to become men like their daddy and my father—the two men I admire most.

—Jennifer Belin

Pensacola, Florida

Nylons and Sixth-Grade Dances

By Madeleine L'Engle

It happens.

It happens suddenly, when you aren't expecting it.

I had always resolved that I would never tell my daughters that they were too old to sit on my lap. Lap sitting hadn't quite ended when my eldest daughter, at the end of her sixth-grade year, was invited to a dance at the regional school where she would be going for junior high.

She was still a little girl. He braids were gone because her younger sister on a dare one morning had cut one off. But she was still a little girl, with straight blond hair and big, innocent eyes. We began talking about what she would wear to the dance. What were the other girls going to wear?

Her younger sister said, "Not a party dress. Kids don't wear party dresses anymore."

What do you wear to your first dance when you are finishing the sixth grade? The children—yes, they were still children—would be driven to the regional school by various parents. It wouldn't be a dance where there were dates. These children had gone through school together; they knew each other. But at the dance there would be boys and girls from two other schools, who would be strangers to them. Who might be more grown up. Who would surely be different.

"Stockings!" our younger daughter exclaimed. "You have to have nylons!"

I didn't have many nylons myself. We lived in a dairy farm village, and I usually wore knee socks and comfortable moccasins. I dug through my drawer for a pair of nylons. My older daughter was only ten. My nylons were much too big for her. They sagged. We tried to pull them up, and it wasn't working.

"Where's Daddy?" our younger daughter asked.

Daddy went into town and brought back a pair of nylons the right size. After phone calls for consultations with friends, we decided on a navy blue skirt and a pretty white blouse.

It's too soon, I thought. It's much too soon.

By the time our younger daughter was finishing sixth grade, we had left our little village and were back in New York, in Manhattan. The school dances were in the school, within easy walking distance. We could get a pair of nylons in a shop just around the corner and across the street. It was still too soon.

Madeleine L'Engle is the bestselling author of *A Wrinkle in Time* and *Mothers and Daughters*.

ELEVEN

Female Frenzy

No relationship is as highly charged as that between mother and daughter, or as riddled with expectations that could, like a land mine, detonate with a single misstep, a solitary stray word that, without a warning, wounds or enrages. And no relationship is as bursting with possibilities of good will and understanding.

—Victoria Secunda

*A daughter and her mother are never free from one another—
no matter how they disagree. For they are so entwined in heart
and mind that, gladly or unwillingly, they share each love, each
joy, each sorrow and each bitter wrong lifelong.*

—Pam Brown

*The daughter never ever gives up on the mother, just as the
mother never gives up on the daughter. There is a tie here so
strong that nothing can break it.*

—Rachel Billington

*What could be more profoundly disturbing and exquisitely joy-
ful than a mother-daughter relationship? What could possibly
be more fraught with the creative combustion of the universe
than two females who were charged with the task of creating
and reflecting each other?*

—Shirley MacLaine

Actress Shirley MacLaine and Sachi in 1959. © Allan Grant/Timepix

Mother of My Mother

By Hope Edelman

My daughter was born on October 13, 1997, pulled out into a dim birthing room in the presence of five adults who badly needed sleep. I hadn't spent those surreal gray hours in a hospital since I was seventeen years old, and I hadn't planned to spend them there again. But this time, instead of the muffled sobs of relatives and the background hum of institutional machines, there was screaming and sweating and swearing and nobody, thankfully, was thinking about death. The first words my daughter heard from her mother were "Is it a girl?" and from her father "I can't tell."

I lifted my head as the doctor propped Maya into a sitting position, her mouth stretched into an angry howl, the slimy, ropy umbilical cord stretching like a purple leash from her stomach back to the birth canal, and I saw the unmistakable crease of skin between her legs. I had the sudden urge to grab the cord and yank the placenta free. The nurse wiped the baby dry and placed her on my chest; I traced the outline of her tiny shoulder blades with my index fingers and tasted her forehead with my tongue. She raised her head and blinked. And at that unforgettable moment, when I might have been awed by the miracle of birth, or apologizing to my husband for punching him in the chest and yelling "I *am* pushing!" as I forced the baby out, or wondering how the hell a newborn could lift its head like that, I was thinking this instead: that my daughter's time of birth missed my mother's time of death by exactly ten minutes on the clock, and thank God my grandmother never knew her first great-grandchild was born on the thirteenth.

They appear like this without warning, my grandmother and my mother, speaking to me in unexpected ways. They act as my domestic Greek chorus, reminding me to light the menorah, make my house presentable for guests, and keep my husband and child well fed. Some would call them my conscience. Yet occasionally they're discordant, continuing to disagree even after death. "Isn't it too chilly to bathe the baby?" my grandmother asks, wringing her hands as I start to fill the tub. "Oh, for God's sake, Mother," my mother says, hands resting on her hips. "The child needs a bath and it's the middle of December. We can't postpone baths all winter." And so I, still trying to be the peacemaker, drag the space heater into the bathroom so Maya can be warm *and* clean, which is, I realize as she splashes happily in the tub, exactly the right compromise to have made.

Women are born twice, the poet Anne Sexton wrote, and I once interpreted that to mean first from their mothers and again through their daughters. But now I think women are born many more times than that, three times, four times, for as long as their maternal lines remain intact. When my husband and I first saw the blurry physical evidence on the ultrasound screen that Maya was a girl, he said, "I don't mean to scare you, but that's where your grandchildren are going to come from." It was both an overwhelming and comforting thought.

We are all inside one another, like the painted wooden Russian matrushka dolls my grandmother bought for me when I was six. I see this with startling clarity now as I watch Maya sitting at her toy piano. She bangs on the keys with her tiny hands and we tunnel together through time. She is a child and I am her mother, she is me and I am my mother, she is my mother and I am my grandmother. This is our family album. My grandmother and my mother live on through my daughter as surely as they live on in me. Listen to her play. They are her inspiration. She is their song.

Hope Edelman is the bestselling author of *Motherless Daughters* and *Mother of My Mother.*

≈

Every mother contains her daughter in herself and every daughter her mother, and every woman extends backwards into her mother and forwards into her daughter.
—C. G. Jung

We are connected throughout time and regardless of place. We are our mothers' daughters.
—Cokie Roberts

My life flows from you, Mama. My style comes from a long line of Louises who picked me up in the night to keep me from wetting the bed. A long line of Sarahs who fed me and my sister and fourteen other children from watery soups and beans and a lot of imagination. A long line of Lizzies who made me understand love.
—Sonia Sanchez

*Sons branch out, but
one woman leads to another.*

Finally, I know you
through your daughter,
my mother, her sisters,
and through myself.

—Margaret Atwood

The Years of Flowing

By Kate Young Caley

I remember that first, bright drop, no bigger than a dime—the red stain on my white underpants was exactly the proof I had been waiting for.

"My daughter," Mom said, smiling, when I told her, "now you are almost a woman." She hugged me and said, "Let's go for a walk, just you and me."

Kate Young Caley with daughters Jennie and Elizabeth.

As we made our way down the field toward the brook that flowed across our land she explained things her own mother had never been comfortable enough to say to her. And I (a bit uncomfortable myself, but glad to be away from the shy smirks of my brothers and father) listened to the story of the day when she first flowed.

She had thought she was bleeding to death. She screamed for my Scottish Presbyterian grandmother, who handed her a bunch of cut-up rags from the back of a drawer. "Here. Use these," my grandmother had said. "You'll need them every month."

Now, remembering the questions that were left unanswered for her that day, my mother walked with me to the edge of our brook to a small waterfall of rocks. One of our favorite spots. We sat down. She told me I could ask her anything.

I wanted to ask her if it would always be this wonderful. Was it this exciting every month? Would I always feel the joy of this day—was *this* what it meant to be a woman? That tiny red drop on my white underpants was one of the most beautiful things I had ever seen. I thought I had been given the secret to the life for which I hoped. Perhaps I had.

It was that first bright drop that let me hope I might one day have babies.

Years later, when I gave birth, first to one daughter and then a few years later to another, each was born so perfect and beautiful. And as I held them I thought of their own eggs hidden deep and whole within those tiny bodies awaiting their day.

And now, so quickly, is the time when I watch them become women. I see their bodies soften and shape with curves like my own body. When we stand together, my daughters and me, people recognize we are related: They can see the mysterious passing of family similarities that flowed through our mothers and grandmothers into each of us.

So many kinds of flowing these days. That is part of now. Flowing and flowing away.

College letters arrive in the mail for my oldest daughter, Elizabeth, trying to lure her from us. I hand them over and watch her open them with such excitement. And I pretend they don't draw blood, the blood of my own unready heart.

And what of my younger girl, Jennie? The one I was counting on to stay the baby? The one who a few weeks ago told me she thought she was getting her period?

"No, sweetie," I replied. "You won't begin your flow until you have pubic hair."

"Mama," she said. "I *have* pubic hair."

How does she know something I don't know?

Wasn't it so very recently that I knew every inch of that little body? A soft face cloth in my own loving hand washed around every little crease of her warm neck, over her toddler belly, and down each chubby, strong leg. So soon now she begins the cycles that will accompany her womanhood. More flowing away.

And just as she commences becoming a woman, I enter the waning of my own cycle. The time is near for my body to cease that monthly rite I've observed since I was just her age.

As my daughters' bodies change into the smooth and firm lines that were also mine before I birthed them, I watch closely. Regard their youth. They are all potential. All possibility.

And if I mourn just a little, just occasionally, for the possibilities that are no longer mine, who, really, could fault me?

But just as my mother did (and all the mothers before her) now I pass on to these daughters—through all of our bodies—the responsibility for future births. It is time for me to let their bodies take them where they might. To let their womanly bodies carry on the work of the women we are and might become.

My own years of flowing, having served me well, will now rest.

Kate Young Caley is the author of *The House Where the Hardest Things Happened.* She is a speaker and workshop leader, and lives with her husband and their two daughters in Quincy, Massachusetts.

A lot of girls for one staircase.

My four little girls . . . born within three years of each other. We've shopped for First Communion dresses, prom dresses, wedding dresses, and maternity dresses. I've cut, brushed, washed, and braided their blond locks of hair; I've refereed their fights over borrowed sweaters, misplaced hairdryers, stolen boyfriends; and I've watched each of them grow into her own beautiful person. Even though we all now live in different towns, I still hold them and their spouses and children in my heart and in my prayers all through the day.

—Nancy J. Guenin
Dayton, Ohio

I am beyond grateful for the times Chelsea and I have circled the globe together. And if those travels have changed minds in countries where daughters are not as prized as sons—well, all the better.

—Hillary Rodham Clinton

Former First Lady Hillary Rodham Clinton and daughter Chelsea visit the Western Wall in 1999. © Ziv Koren/Polaris Images

Daughters, I have discovered, can be wonderful allies, good friends, co-conspirators, and a mother's greatest delight. We have laughed together, cried together, played together, fought together, and always loved together. Through the best of times and the worst of times, we have emerged as friends. I am truly blessed and grateful for having had the privilege of sharing their lives and watching them grow and mature into the unique women they are today.

—Kathleen R. Moore

Arnold, Maryland

Interlude ❧

Comedienne/actress Joan Rivers with daughter
Melissa. © Acey Harper/Timepix

Graduation Day
By Joan Rivers

Restoring my relationship with Melissa after Edgar's
death was a long and often agonizing process. By the time

she returned to college for her senior year, we were enjoying each other's company; and when graduation neared, she told me that her classmates wanted me to speak at the ceremony.

And so I addressed her college graduating class of the University of Pennsylvania. I told a few jokes and gave the graduates the usual commencement advice. But there was nothing usual about the way I felt on that graduation day. My daughter had been through more pain in two years than any woman deserves in a lifetime, and she had come through. Not only had she graduated with her class on time, but she had graduated with honors. Even more important, she had retained her kind and sensitive heart.

When I finished my speech, I looked into the audience and saw Melissa and the friends who had helped her though the last two years. Few events on earth are more moving than a college graduation. Melissa and her friends looked so brave and confident as they prepared to head into the big scary world. And I knew that waiting for them were sharks that belonged in *Jaws.* These kids would need so much courage and luck. They would have to be a new batch of Winston Churchill's disciples. I hoped that some of them were aware that *I* had never given up.

"I love you, Melissa," I suddenly said, as if the two of us were alone, and she answered by blowing me a kiss from her seat. I was so overwhelmed by joy and pride and relief that we had found our way back to each other that I could barely hold myself together long enough to leave the podium.

And then the entire class rose and gave me a standing

ovation. My stand-up career should have ended right there, for knocking 'em dead at Buckingham Palace would have been just a lounge act compared to this. Of course, this was the first applause I'd ever gotten that wasn't really for me. It was for my daughter.

Joan Rivers is an award-winning actress and author of *Bouncing Back.*

TWELVE

They Eventually Grow Up

Your children are not your children.
They are the sons and daughters of
Life's longing for itself.
They come through you but not from you,
And though they are with you, they belong not to you.
You may give them your love but not your thoughts.
For they have their own thoughts.
You may house their bodies but not their souls,

For their souls dwell in the house of tomorrow,
Which you cannot visit, not even in your dreams.
You may strive to be like them,
But seek not to make them like you.
For life goes not backward nor tarries with yesterday.
You are the bows from which your children
As living arrows are sent forth.

—Kahlil Gibran

It's always been my feeling that God lends you your children
until they're about eighteen years old.

—Betty Ford

The Empty Nest

By Susan Heyboer O'Keefe

"It was the worst time of my life."

"I couldn't stop crying."

"I thought I was going crazy."

These were empty-nest mothers, trying to prepare me for my college-bound son's leaving home. I clucked knowingly at their comments, confident *I* wasn't going to be as pathetic as they were. Didn't they have husbands, friends, jobs? Didn't they have lives of their own?

Being a parrot lover, I jokingly said, "I know the perfect thing to do with an empty nest. I'm going to fill it with birds! I'll turn the empty bedroom into an aviary."

During my son's senior year in high school, I lived life as normally as life can ever be lived, looked forward to some long-deserved peace and quiet, and remained in deepest denial.

Shortly after his high school graduation, I began to cry. I kept on crying. I thought I was going crazy. It was one of the worst times of my life.

How could I possibly live for months on end without my son, who is not just my only child but also a creative, funny, and thoughtful person I treasure for his own sake? It was unnatural!

My solution was to suggest that he go to the local community college, where at least, when my anticipated end-of-the-world earthquake hit, I could walk to get him. My husband's solution was more complicated: Simply enroll himself at the same college and be our son's roommate. Each of us mentioned our idea; neither of us laughed.

At one point I realized with horror that this wasn't going to be just a few semesters' separation relieved by vacations and breaks. Girls came home after college; boys often moved directly from dorms to apartments of their own. So this was really forever. My end-of-the-world fears escalated, and I wept through the rest of the summer. The day my husband and I drove our son to campus and dropped him off, I outright bawled.

My unpredictable tears were just beginning to dry when September 11 hit. We live in New Jersey with a view of New York City, the smoke from the destroyed Twin Towers visible from most of town. My son was hours away near Philadelphia, far beyond walking distance. Immediate rumors said that Philly was one of the next targets. I sat by the television, unable to get a phone connection to the college, as my irrational fear—this dreadful, unnamable, end-of-the-world act—played out before my eyes.

So much true tragedy happened on September 11. I don't mean to trivialize it in any way by lumping my neurotic fears in with the real grief and shock of those directly affected. But my emotions at both events are forever intertwined for me: getting through to the college at last, hearing my son's voice as my fingers dug into the phone receiver, weeping for the victims while weeping with personal gratitude and relief. Was my son ever in real danger? It doesn't matter. I thought he was, and that's the same thing to a mother's heart.

The many lessons an empty nester must learn over time were taught to me in one grueling session: to appreciate my child even more with the distance, to trust in his maturity and good sense, and to let go because—and here's the hardest lesson—I never really had control in the first place.

My son is a twice-given gift. I was given him at birth, and I was given him again, in a way, on September 11.

Like many people, I have tried to live more consciously since then. I know I am more keenly aware of how grateful I am that my son is who he is. He's always made me proud, but in his absence this pride swells. There's also more than a bit of amazement at how well he's doing. I can't believe that the same teenager who could never get up on his own makes it to an 8:30 ancient Greek class every morning.

As I write, it is now late March of the academic year that began so tearfully. I eventually stopped crying over both sources of sorrow. Time, of course, is the great healer. My own situation has had the additional help of having one of the world's chattiest kids—and the phone bills to prove it. We seem to talk as much if not more than before. Or perhaps it only feels that way since our conversations have been stripped of the "What are we having for supper? Can I get a ride? Where's my blue shirt?" filler of living together. We speak more as equals; at the same time I think he's more willing to ask for advice than he was while living at home. Before, my husband and I knew everything that was happening in his world and we gave our opinions, usually unasked. Now we have to be told everything, and in his telling us, "What do you think?" often follows.

The wound of separation is beginning to close. I felt this the first time he came home on break, lugging fifty pounds of dirty clothes despite my strict instructions to use the dorm laundry before we picked him up. Getting a smelly whiff from the opened duffel bag, I wanted to use tongs rather than my hands to sort things, and I got angrier still. But the anger was good. It meant I had gone past feeling "my greatly missed beloved son can do no wrong" to healthier emotions.

Regaining my sense of humor also signaled a return to normalcy. I discovered many unsuspected benefits of being an empty-nest mother, such as one less male to hog the remote. Oh, and the mystery of the spontaneous evaporation of milk has suddenly solved itself.

I haven't yet turned my son's room into an aviary. After all, he's still home on breaks and will be back for summers, and he won't necessarily be moving out after graduation, or so I now tell myself. More, the sheer clutter I'd have to clean first is overwhelming. The room is littered wall-to-wall with clothes, books, and CDs (and that's just the stuff he left behind). Not a single inch of floor is visible. Any change that doesn't involve a blowtorch would be near impossible to make. And I think that, though I'm content, for now I've had change enough.

Susan Heyboer O'Keefe is the author of a dozen picture books and the new young adult novel, *My Life and Death by Alexandra Canarsie.*

There's something so bittersweet about your children going off to college. You're thrilled that they've gotten into good schools, but you also know it's a passage in life and that life will never be the same. That they've grown up.

—Laura Bush

Laura Bush with daughters Barbara
and Jenna at Inaugural Ball in 2001.
© Larry Downing/Reuters/Timepix

When mothers talk about the depression of the empty next, they're not mourning the passing of all those wet towels on the floor, or the music that numbs your teeth, or even the bottles of capless shampoo dribbling down the shower drain. They're upset because they've gone from supervisor of a child's life to spectator. It's like being the vice president of the United States.

—Erma Bombeck

In the first quiet moments with my daughter, the day after her birth, I stared down at my first and only child and whispered to her: "Well, little baby, I'm giving you the next eighteen years of my life. You may have my time, energy, love, and devotion unconditionally. Whatever you need, I'll be there for you, no matter what, no questions asked."

Amazingly, that eighteen-year commitment is nearing completion. Obviously, I will love Molly with all my heart for the rest of my life—and I will always be there for her—but I knew from my own life that the first eighteen years are when

Martha Flanagan and daughter Molly.

moms are needed the most. As Molly grew older, I became less of a playmate and more of a confidante. Then confidante evolved into counselor as the influence of friends during the high school years became more central and important in her life. Now year 17 rushes toward 18, and preparations for the transition to college have begun. The role of mom again is undergoing a change. Conversations are more adultlike. Decisions on classes are focused on getting into the college that is right for her and for her career beyond. Discussions about relationships with the young men and the young women in her life demonstrate wisdom beyond her years.

And what is now so apparent: My "little baby" has grown up.

—Martha Flanagan
Cincinnati, Ohio

The Best Stage of All

By LaVonne Neff

Every now and then, usually right after a major holiday, my husband and I look at each other and say, "You know, we should have had more kids."

As it is, we have two daughters, now in their early thirties. When they were in their terrible twos or interesting teens, we thought we had quite enough children, thank you. And we never felt that we spent too little for their college educations. What we wish we had is more *grown* children.

When I was twenty-seven, visiting the small town

LaVonne Neff with daughters
Heidi and Molly.

where I went to high school, I phoned the mother of one of
my close friends. We updated each other: I now had two
children, and my friend was working in Germany, and her
little brother (who, last time I saw him, was trying to get a
pair of hamsters to mate on the dining table) had become a
computer expert. "It's so nice to have grown-up children,"
my friend's mother said. "You don't have to worry about
them."

I was startled. As the daughter and daughter-in-law of
women who, as we say in our family, exercise the ministry
of intercessory worry, I could hardly believe my ears. I called
my mother to share this amazing philosophy. "I disagree,"
my mother firmly said. "You worry about your kids your
whole life."

Indeed she did, but I decided to make an effort to

adopt my friend's mother's approach instead. I am not entirely successful—for example, when Heidi, my younger daughter, moved to New Orleans, then known as America's murder capital, and insisted on walking places after dark unescorted, I had to remind myself that worry was no longer required. Fortunately, I soon learned that she had thought things through: "If I feel uneasy," she told me, "I just start singing loudly. No one wants to mess with a crazy woman."

The best way, I've found, to turn off worry before it grabs me and starts sucking my breath is to remember what I was doing and how I was feeling when I was whatever age my daughters are now. Somehow it seems odd to hover protectively over people who are the age I was when my friends and I began talking about midlife crises.

It also helps to consider where the kids may have gotten some of their foolhardy ideas. When Molly, my older daughter, told me she was planning to have her first baby at home with two lay midwives in attendance, I had to take a very deep breath. But then I realized that, as usual, the apple was falling pretty close to the tree. At her age I was teaching Lamaze classes, and she—still in diapers—was demonstrating the exercises to my enthralled students. By now Molly has had three healthy babies at home, and I have completely stopped hyperventilating.

Long ago a *Readers Digest* article made a huge impression on me. Children should be raised so that they truly are adults when they legally become so, it said. By age eighteen, young adults should be self-supporting, responsible for their own debts and decisions. Teach the little birdies to fly and then shove them out of the nest. I must have been thinking of that article when Heidi asked me, "What would you do if, after college, I needed to come home to live for a while?" "Buy a smaller house," I said.

That is not strictly true, but I am grateful that my children want to stand on their own two feet. It is much easier to see someone as an adult if you're not sending support checks or getting into arguments over the mess in her bedroom, just as it is much easier to *be* an adult if you have your own home and pay your own bills. It's so nice—for them as well as for me—that I no longer have to worry about their clothes, their friends, their diet, their pastimes, and what time they come home at night. And freed from the ties that bind, grown-up kids can be really good friends.

When I brought my first baby home from the hospital, I had one late-night moment of terror. Until she left for college, I thought, I would never get a full night's sleep, never read a book, probably never even wash my hair. Fortunately I was no prophet. I quickly learned that life would go on, often quite happily, and that each stage was more pleasant than the last. Call me weird, but I do enjoy adolescents more than toddlers. And grown-up children are the most fun of all.

LaVonne Neff is the author of many articles and several books, including *One of a Kind: Making the Most of Your Child's Uniqueness.* She and husband David live in Illinois, which (she believes) should be moved closer to Texas and California, homes of their two daughters, son-in-law, and three grandchildren.

❧

Thank you for showing me, when I thought my mothering days were over, that the best days between us are only just beginning.
—Pam Brown

Being a mom also means being a grandma. The thing I enjoy most about being a mom is the continual look of awe in the eyes of my kids, and now in the eyes of my grandkids: their first barefoot walk in the grass, their first time seeing snow, and all of the other firsts in their lives. As old as my kids are now, I still see that look in their eyes when their kids do, say, or see something new for the first time.

—Jackie Fledderman
Batesville, Indiana

I don't know exactly when I realized that my biological clock was ticking, but I was in my mid-fifties when our neighbors' young children began to come over to visit me without their mothers. We were living out of the country without other family members nearby, and everybody treated each other as relatives, celebrating birthdays and holidays together. So I didn't think it was unusual when I had little visitors.

Then we retired and returned to the United States, moving next door to a nice young couple who were expecting their first baby. My husband and I remarked that it was going to be such fun to watch a little one grow up nearby, as our own grown and married children live across the country and haven't yet had their own babies.

We offered to keep little David a few hours each week so his stay-at-home mom could go out for a swim. That's when it hit me: My grandmother-wanna-be clock was banging loudly! This past year has been a joyful one, watching him develop from a tiny, snuggly newborn into a happy, confident toddler with a mind of his own. I still melt when he arrives at our door and flashes that big smile. Of course, we're eagerly looking forward to having our own biological grandchildren, but David will always have a special place in our family. Being a surro-gate grandmother is great!

—Anne Grawemeyer
Louisville, Kentucky

My two granddaughters have given me more than just the chance to be a grandmother, the opportunity to experience some of the precious moments that I did not have with my own two daughters.

—Marcella K. Hsiung
Cincinnati, Ohio

Grandchildren soften our hearts. They loosen the sludge of old resentments and regrets. It's a chance for reconciliation between ourselves and our children.

—Gail Sheehy

Interlude 🌿

Biological Baloney
By Jane Leavy

People ask all the time whether I'd feel any differently about Nick and Emma if they were my "own" children. I always reply that I can't conceive of it—which is pointed as well as true. It's impossible to imagine loving them more if they were of me. I mean, I love their father and the cat and the dog, and we don't share the same DNA.

There is only one sense in which I feel they are not mine—the proprietary one. I do not possess them. Rather I am possessed by them, an irrevocable transaction that occurred the moment our eyes met. There are pictures in our family album of me waiting for Nick, a supplicant reclining in a hotel bed, waiting for my life to change. Then came the knock on the door. And I was down on all fours with him: engaged. I cannot remember getting there. I cannot visualize moving from the unmade bed to the carpeted floor. But in that instant, my posture in life changed forever—from passive to active, from mine to theirs. Sadness was banished. A joyous new fact of life was *a priori* true.

Once you have a child in your arms, you stop thinking about all that went before: the envy, the fear, the humiliations; postcoital tests, injections, inseminations, failures. It's all gone. You no longer worry about what it is to be a mother or how to become one because you're too busy being one. Your child supplants your pain.

My children are my teachers. They have taught me to reject the foolishness of genetic hubris. Because of them, I am a more democratic person. Because they are not of me, I do not regard them as tabula rasa on which to inscribe my dreams and expectations. Nick and Emma are the authors of themselves.

Something else: I no longer believe you become a mother with a knock on the door, a call in the night, or even seventeen hours of labor. It's an ongoing process. I am always, and still, becoming their mother.

Jane Leavy is the bestselling author of *Sandy Koufax: A Lefty's Legacy,* a biography of the great Dodgers pitcher, and *Squeeze Play,* a comic novel about life as a female sportswriter.

THIRTEEN

Call Me Mom

Biology is the least of what makes someone a mother.
—Oprah Winfrey

Stepmother

By Alex Witchel

The sum total of my stepmother fantasy came from *The Sound of Music*. While I certainly aspired to wear designer evening gowns and wield a cigarette holder like the baroness and would have loved to play the guitar and be handy enough to make puppets and play clothes like Maria the enterprising nun, I fell, with a thud, somewhere in between. Growing up the eldest of four children—the younger two being ten and thirteen years my junior—I was used to being a surrogate mom. I could only assume that my future stepsons, Nat, ten, and Simon, five, would resemble my two younger brothers—perpetually hungry bathroom hoggers who, once wrenched from either kitchen or shower, spent their time playing sports and reading comic books.

I was close. Everything but the bathroom hogging, because we had a spare. They were terrific boys, smart and funny. Yes, Nat was a little shy and Simon cheated at Monopoly, but mostly they were good company. I had no desire to engage in any tug-of-war with their mother over emotional supremacy. It was enough for me to have a fulfilling marriage to Frank, their father, and hope that as we all got older, the kids would appreciate the benefit of having an extra adult handy who loved them no matter what. Even though as a child that's all you seem surrounded by, once you're grown up you realize that those people are a vanishing breed.

At our wedding, I fed Frank a forkful of cake and did

the same with the boys. They opened their mouths wide and blushed. Everyone applauded.

Most women get a little more adjustment time. You marry and feel all gooey. You get pregnant and feel like a house until you have the baby and feel all gooey again. Then you have another one, but this time you cut your hair because it's easier and who needs makeup, anyway? You learn to carry the extra ten pounds that have somehow appeared with humor and grace and elastic waistbands. And if your kids barely look up from the TV when you're all dolled up on a Saturday night, that's okay, too, as long as the sitter knows where to find you and there are snacks in the fridge.

But becoming a stepmother is instant. I never gave bottles or changed diapers. I joined the party late. Everyone else was right on schedule. It was mine that needed accelerating.

The first year was hard. Simon was used to sleeping in the same bed with his dad from the "bachelor apartment," as they called it, and Nat had only recently graduated to his own territory on the couch. They had always spent each weekend with Dad and they continued to in our new apartment, where they shared a room. For the first six weeks, when we tucked the boys in, Frank would say, "Knock if you need us," and every single time, there was a knock on the door and it would be Simon. Sometimes he had a stomachache, sometimes he had a headache, sometimes he had a bad dream. All times, his dad brought him into bed and told him to lie down and rest awhile. Simon would then fall asleep, as he was used to doing with his daddy beside him, and Frank would carry him back to his bed, where he would wake up the next morning safe and sound.

It occurred to me, on the day I basted the chicken five

times in ten minutes, that I was hiding. I was simply terrified of making more mistakes. Of saying the all-time dreadful thing that would leave the mark of the Wicked
Stepmother upon them. I had worked with a woman once
who called her stepmother Stepmonster. I didn't want that
to happen to me.

It didn't. We got used to each other. We had good
conversations ("An A in math? I'm so proud of you!"), boring conversations ("No, I don't know where your bus pass
is"), and bad conversations ("You *knew* your curfew was
one A.M.!").

As time went on, I came to realize that the situation was
this: The Nat and Simon Corporation had a president and
a chairman of the board—their mother and father. Though
they were no longer married, this was a business arrangement that would never be dissolved. I was a consultant, al-
beit highly placed, whose two cents were considered in the
mix, but who never made the final decision. Which was
okay with me. The important thing was the way their father
treated me, which taught the kids how to treat me. In the
beginning, if I said no to something, they would immediately look to Dad. "Alex said no," he would respond defin-
itively, and that was that.

I also learned when to say no, how to say no, why to say
no. I learned to say "I'm sorry" when I was wrong. I learned
never to walk into their bedroom without knocking (they
returned the favor), to say at the dinner table "Why don't
you try using your knife?" instead of "What are you, an animal?" and to be extra nice on the phone when girls called.
I also learned how to look the other way at parent-teacher
nights when first wives gave me dirty looks when their husbands gave me interested looks and when the teachers

shook my hand, smiling pleasantly though clearly confused at who I was and what I was doing there.

Nat is in college now. He is so tall that when he puts his arm around me I fit under his armpit. Simon is in high school. Last summer we had our first vacation without Nat—he had his own busy schedule, so Frank and I took Simon to a resort hotel in Scottsdale, Arizona, where he gloried in the attention lavished solely upon him.

One day for lunch, we went to the local Ed Debevic's, a branch of the Chicago institution that is a parody of a 1950s' diner: waiters and waitresses in costumes straight out of *Grease* who jump up on the counter to sing and dance. Simon loves it because when they're not performing, the help is notoriously rude. They sit at your table and insult you—about your "square outfit" or "low IQ" if you have a question about the food.

We sat down and reviewed the menu . . . and were eagerly making a list of all our favorite dishes as the waitress approached. Bleached blonde, a biker-chick type. I steeled myself for the onslaught. But as she came closer her face softened.

"Hello, little family," she said gently, almost wistfully. Simon looked up at her and smiled. Frank started to order. I glowed.

Alex Witchel is a reporter in the "Style" department of *The New York Times* and the author of *Girls Only: Sleepovers, Squabbles, Tuna Fish and Other Facts of Family Life.* She and her husband live in New York City.

❧

One of the things I like best about watercolor painting is watching the different colors flow into each other. There's always an element of surprise as gravity works its magic in pulling one shade into another. Sometimes the new combination of colors creates an explosion of sunset orange or a lake sapphire blue. Other times, especially when the complementary colors of orange and blue, red and green, or yellow and purple mix and meld, the result may be a beautiful shade of gray.

A stepmother's palette is loaded with all kinds of colors. At times it's difficult to know whether I should dip my brush into a fiery cadmium red or a calming sap green. Like painting, stepmothering takes all the passion, patience, and creativity I can muster. Certain skills and a dollop or two of wisdom go a long way toward creating a pleasing picture.

When I first started painting, I slathered on all the brightest colors I had with the intention of creating something that was vibrant and full of life. And in 1989, when I first became a stepmother, I applied my enthusiasm for this new family unit, envisioning our stepfamily bursting with fresh life and energy. Little did I realize that this renascent life and energy would, like a bold splash of watercolor, create unforeseen results that were not always pleasant or desirable.

It was time for my lesson in grays. With a mind-set of "mine" and "yours," you get an "ours" that is as dull and flat as a watercolor gray mixed from sooty black and chalky white. But grays mixed from complementary colors are another story—or painting. These grays retain their vibrancy and integrity while contributing to a new, blended hue.

For me the greatest joy of living in a stepfamily comes when we honor all the complementary colors that contribute to it. Easier said than done. I have discovered, however, that if I allow each color the freedom to be itself and give it some space to run and blend into other hues, I am more likely to end up with a vibrant painting.

—Patricia Donohoe
Shepherdstown,
West Virginia

Made for Each Other

By Suzanne Muldoon

*E*very mother of a two-year-old becomes exasperated at the constant chorus of demands that come with being called Mommy. But I never tire of hearing the word "Mommy," because for some time I thought motherhood was out of the realm of possibility for me.

After unsuccessful attempts at getting pregnant, my husband and I sought a variety of treatments—a series of doctor visits and surgeries. I began to feel singled out from women who were allowed to become mothers, as though the life that I had envisioned for myself was out of my reach. My story was the one every infertile woman shares: the painful Mother's Days, the pangs of jealousy when a friend announced a pregnancy, the feelings of inadequacy and confusion.

At one point in the treatments, the doctor thought that he had discovered the source of the problem and believed that he would be able to overcome it by certain procedures. During the time in which my husband and I were waiting for the result of the treatment, we traveled to a conference. When I got to the hotel, I found an article in *St. Louis*

Magazine about a couple's journey to China to adopt their daughter. It scared me. I went to the mall and saw several Caucasian couples with Asian children. "How nice for them," I thought, "but I want to be pregnant!" I returned to the hotel and saw another mixed race family. At that point, my heart told me what I did not want to hear. My answer would not be pregnancy; it would be in China. I grieved when the tests confirmed that I was not pregnant.

When all of the treatments failed, I told a friend that I felt ready to adopt. Although I wanted a Chinese baby, it seemed so impossible. For one, we were told we were too young and had to wait five years, and we did not have the money that was required to travel there. Why did I feel that my child was in China if I could not figure out how to get her?

However, one month later the laws changed and the money arrived from an unexpected source. We began to hope again for the first time in years. The night before we left for China, my husband and I rented a Chinese movie and got some take-out Chinese food. We joked that the fortune cookie might say something like "You will travel to a far land and find a daughter." When I read my fortune, I began sobbing so furiously that my husband thought I might be fooling him. I handed him the fortune that said, "Happier days are definitely ahead for you, struggle has ended."

I knew that it was true. My tears were a release of the pain from our wait and the sense of a new hope.

On December 11, 2000, in a hotel room in Anhui, China, I became a mom. A beautiful ten-month-old named Zhu Dian Dian was placed into my arms. I immediately felt heartbreak, not the overwhelming joy that I had anticipated. She was keenly aware that something major was happening and cried a deep, soulful cry. I rocked her and consoled her. I cried a little with her. I realize now that crying with her instead of being overjoyed for myself was the essence of becoming her mom. It was not about what I wanted to fulfill my life, but what would make this beautiful little girl happy.

She cheered up quickly. She was completely captivated by her dad's silly antics and loved to climb all over both of us. She eventually calmed down and fell asleep for the night. When she woke up the next morning, we expected her be panicked upon finding herself in unfamiliar surroundings. But she gave us a huge smile that clearly said, "Oh! It's you two. I'm glad you're still here!" That moment was like the moment when any mother sees her child for the first time. I knew that she was the love of my life and would be mine forever.

In our first few days together, many young Chinese women—waitresses, shopkeepers, and hotel workers—fussed and fawned over her and wanted to hold her. I knew that they would seem more familiar to her than I would. However, after the first week, Grace turned back, reached, and cried for me when I passed her to a lovely woman in a shop we frequented. That might be a normal experience for every mother, but it was quite simply the best moment of my life. I was her mom.

It would be this way for the next seven months. My daughter would not let anyone hold her other than my husband or me. Even when she started to walk, she would pull me along with her so that I was not too far away. Though I never carried her inside my body, I was physically attached to her in the first part of our lives together. I had a great need *to be* a mommy and Grace had a great need *for* a mommy, so we were a perfect match. We were both healed through our time together and our love for each other.

This process of healing is unique to adoptive mothering. Like biological mothers, adoptive mothers experience the joys of seeing their children grow and thrive, but those moments also heal the wounds of a journey to motherhood. Buying baby clothes, going to the park, and participating in playgroups are all experiences that wash away the pain of loss and longing with wonderful new memories.

Suzanne Muldoon is a licensed professional counselor. She lives with her daughter and husband in Indiana, Pennsylvania.

❧

Am I his "real" mother? My guess is that I must feel mighty real to Luc, just as he cannot feel anything but real to me.

—Marcelle Clements
New York, New York

My daughter and I would be splashing in the tub—I loved taking baths with her—and I said, "There are two ways mommies have babies. Sometimes they carry them in their tummy"—I know "tummy" is politically incorrect today, but that's what I said—"and sometimes a mommy can't carry a baby in her tummy. So she carries hers in her heart. You were adopted, so you were born in my heart."

—Barbara Walters

I am the mother of three biological children and three adopted children from Korea. I have known the joy of carrying a child in my womb and then giving birth to her and all the emotions that go along with that wonderful experience. I have also known the joy of waiting for the arrival of my children from the other side of the world and all the emotions that go along with that wonderful experience. I worried as I waited for them to arrive, if I would bond with these children that I had not nurtured in my womb.

When they staggered in from the plane, the bonding with our little three-year-old was almost instantaneous, but, although I fell immediately in love with the nine-month-old, she remained aloof and somewhat detached. She had been in an orphanage since she was born and had been left alone in her crib most of her life. She had little use for us other than to be fed and changed. Then came the evening, about two months after she arrived, when she ran a fever and did not feel very well. It was close to dinnertime and no one was home except me and the little girls. I sat in the rocking chair to hold the baby and try to comfort her until her fever came down. As usual she was stiff in my arms as I sat and rocked her. Then, after about ten minutes, she heaved a heavy sigh and melted into my arms. At that moment she seemed to give up her resistance and let me love her; I started to cry. I sat there for about an hour letting her sister run all around me so I could enjoy the wonder of the moment. From that moment on the bond between us was forged, and it has been a deep, abiding love for the past twenty years.

—Kathleen R. Moore
Arnold, Maryland

Forever Mom

By Patsy Major

One morning a few days after his eighth birthday, I picked up my grandson, Charlie, from his stepmother's door. He was waiting for me, with a black plastic bag for his clothes and a carrier bag of his favorite things. As I drove him home to start his new life with my husband Eric and me, I realized I had become a mother again.

Eric predicted Charlie's fate only a few days after the tiny scrap of a boy was born to my eldest daughter, whose marriage had been a disaster. As we walked to the nursery to visit the baby for the first time, he said to me, "We will end up with this little mite."

So, at the age of forty-seven, I adopted a wee timid, hurt, bewildered boy, our grandson, and made him our own son. I became a full-time mother again, after raising four children.

Actually, I first became a mother at age eleven, when my mom had her second set of babies, her "second family," as she referred to them. I helped in many ways, picking up the younger ones from nursery school and caring for them until Mummy got home. As my father's business grew, so did my responsibilities. I became a second mother to my younger sister and brother.

Then I grew up and became the mother of three daughters and a son. I have experienced much joy, but also sadness, in raising them.

When they were all young, I would sometimes stand at their bedsides as they slept. As I bent down to give a gentle good night kiss, I would cry and want to hold off the world from them in case they were hurt, which often they were.

I loved the days we went off to family picnics, food cooked and packed, journeys planned. The holidays were special times when I could renew my friendships with the children.

I loved their teen years. The house always seemed full of young people. Paul, our son, more often than not came home after school with his pal. They would eat a whole loaf of bread, spread thickly with peanut butter, before settling down to do their homework. The smell of peanut butter even today brings back all those happy hours in our kitchen. The girls' boyfriends always passing though . . . the tears of lost loves . . . the dressing for that special party. They were happy and hectic times. The astonishment when the whiskey bottle only held cold tea! Did we do the same to our parents? Yes.

Round three of motherhood—after the practice session with my younger siblings and raising my own four—is much different. Charlie has filled me with happiness and made me to feel young. I have found new friends from the younger mums at the Parents' Association meeting. We went back to bucket and spade holidays, where we spent endless hours at the beach, building sand castles and playing in the water. We visited Disney World. And we have laughed so much in the years we've had Charlie that it has almost made up for all the tears and hurt caused by our daughter's turning her back on her son.

All the worries, the hard work, and the tears have been a mere nothing as we prepare our grandson to go off to college and make his own way in the world. We can now look forward to a life with just the two of us a little later than we had planned and to spending more time with our grand-daughters.

I have had an unexpectedly full life as a mother three different times in my life. And I will always be one. I can't think of anything I'd rather do.

Patsy Major is the mother of five children, including her adopted grandson. She lives in the United Kingdom.

⊶

Being a day care mom has afforded me an endless supply of hugs, kisses, and "I love yous." Each child knows that I am there for him or her—through diaper changes, runny noses, new teeth, separation anxiety from their biological moms, potty training, and the terror of their first days of school. I am that

"Sue Mama" with her 9-to-5 kids.

mom—they call me "Sue Mama"—who doesn't let them get away with too much, but who is willing to reward great accomplishments and good behavior with a trip to the zoo, a visit to the park, or walking and lunch at the mall.

I've learned that each child is different, and that is good. Each child has to be treated as himself or herself—not compared to another child his or her same age. Patience is not only a virtue, it's a must as a mother. And I've learned that children really like structure and discipline, as long as it is done lovingly and with positive reinforcement.

I have only one regret. I wish that I had kept a list of all the children that I have day-cared for. Some came while Mom and Dad were working out a marital concern, while others had a mom who worked part time. But by far the most names on the list would come from children whose moms worked full time and trusted me with their care. The longest that I worked for one family was thirteen years, through four children. As you might suspect, I'm at the point in my life where I have had the chance to day-care for the children of my original day care children. I've also had the opportunity to take part in numerous graduations and several weddings of former day care children.

I believe that I have been truly blessed to be a part of the lives of so many young children. Today I am asked if I am the grandma of my little group of children, rather than the mom. But the results are the same—a love of mothering that has spanned a couple of decades and allowed me to look into the eyes and hearts of some of tomorrow's leaders.

This mother couldn't ask for anything better. And at the end of each day I thank God for giving me the greatest gift that He had available: motherhood.

—Sue Johnson
Waterford, Wisconsin

To our surrogate moms, thank you for your selflessness, your courage, and your generosity. Thank you for your willingness to help us grow and blossom, even though we came to you from soil that was not your own. Thank you for so gently transplanting us into your lives and for being there when we needed you most.

—Kristin Clark Taylor
Great Falls, Virginia

Interlude ❧

I still love making movies, but I take more pride in my role as a mother and a wife.

—Michelle Pfeiffer

Motherhood is the greatest thing I've ever done. This is the greatest thing I'll ever do.

—Kim Basinger

My first job is to be a good mother.

—Faye Dunaway

Faye Dunaway and child.
© O'Neill Terry/Corbis Sygma

This is the biggest performance I've ever done, having this child and being his mother.

—Vivian Banks

When people ask me what I do, I always say I am a mother first. Your children represent your thoughts. Your children are a statement.

—Jacqueline Jackson

I am going to put on my tombstone "Motherhood."

—Diana Ross

FOURTEEN

Mom in Culture

The Ten Best TV Shows about Motherhood You'll Ever Watch

By Ellen Leventry

There's nothing more American than Mom, apple pie, and TV sitcoms. Whether it's June Cleaver with her baked goods or Roseanne with her biting sarcasm, small-screen mothers reflect the world of their off-screen counterparts with warmth, strength, and humor. With that in mind, here are my picks of some of the best.

TV sitcom mom June Cleaver
with her clan. © Universal Studios

1. *Leave It to Beaver* (1957–1963, CBS/ABC)

The quintessential sitcom mom, June Cleaver (Barbara Billingsley) is the mother whom all others are measured against, television and real world. Looking fabulous in her pearls, she always had a fresh batch of cookies waiting after school for Wally (Tony Dow) and the Beaver (Jerry Mathers), and graciously put up with their ever-present friends, Eddie Haskell and Whitey.

2. *Happy Days* (1974–1984, ABC)

Marion Cunningham (Marion Ross) was the neighborhood mom you always wanted to have. Known affectionately as Mrs. C, she reared Richie (Ron Howard), Joanie, and eldest son Chuck, and acted as a surrogate parent to an ever-increasing brood of characters: Arthur "Fonzie" Fonzarelli, Ralph, Chachi, and Warren "Potsie" Weber, plus assorted nephews and nieces. A devoted and dutiful housewife,

184 I Love Being a Mom

Mrs. C maintained her motherly moxie by telling her husband to "sit on it" from time to time.

3. The Brady Bunch (1969–1974, ABC)

Long before *Once and Again,* Carol Ann Brady (played by Florence Henderson) was watching over TV's favorite blended family. When widower Mike Brady (Robert Reed) asks widow Carol to marry him, they must figure out a way to meld her three girls—Marcia (Maureen McCormick), Jan (Eve Plumb), and Cindy (Susan Olsen)—and his three boys—Greg (Barry Williams), Peter (Christopher Knight), and Bobby (Mike Lookinland)—into one happy family. Whether it was the measles, braces, or cursed tiki statues, this "lovely lady" treated every one of the bunch as her very own.

4. The Simpsons (1989–, FOX)

Many sitcom characters have been accused of being two-dimensional, but in the case of Marjorie Bouvier Simpson (voiced by Julie Kavner), it happens to be true. Perhaps one of the longest-suffering television matriarchs, Marge is not only mother to precocious Bart, genius Lisa, and laconic Maggie, but also to doughnut-munching, drooling husband Homer. Putting her own aspirations aside—she has been a policewoman, a pretzel vendor, and even an amateur bowler—Marge is always there for her family with morally sound advice and unconditional love, making her more dimensional than many live-action characters on TV.

5. Roseanne (1988–1997, ABC)

A groundbreaking depiction of a caring, though acerbic, working-class mother, Roseanne ran for nine successful seasons. Whether working in a plastics factory or a beauty salon, or running her own diner, Roseanne Connor (Roseanne) labored tirelessly so that her kids—depressed Darlene, blond Becky, and youngest D.J.—could have a better future. Unlike other sitcom moms, Roseanne didn't have the answer to all of her children's problems, and issues were rarely resolved by the end of an episode.

6. *One Day at a Time* (1975–1984, CBS)

While not the first divorced mother on television (Vivian Bagley, *The Lucy Show),* Ann Romano embodied the real-life struggles of many newly single women of the late 1970s. After seventeen years of marriage, Romano, played by Bonnie Franklin, found herself attempting to reenter the workplace, raising two constantly combative teens, Julie (Mackenzie Phillips) and Barbara (Valerie Bertinelli), and battling her deadbeat ex-husband for child support, while fending off the advances of the building superintendent, Dwayne Schneider (Pat Harrington, Jr).

7. *The Cosby Show* (1984–1992, NBC)

As Claire Huxtable, Phylicia Rashad redefined the typical sitcom mom. She was a lawyer, she was an African American, and she was an equal partner in the decision-making, child-rearing process with her husband Cliff Huxtable (Bill Cosby). The more authoritarian of the two, she handled the trials of Sandra, Denise, Theo, Vanessa, and Rudy with love and all deliberate speed.

8. *The Partridge Family* (1970–1974, ABC)

No whining about having to take the minivan in this family, as Mom was the chauffeur of one very psychedelic tour bus. This show makes the cut not only for Shirley Jones's portrayal of hip 1970s' popstar/supermom Shirley Partridge, but because real-life stepson David Cassidy played her television son Keith. Rounding out the musical family were Laurie (Susan Dey), Danny (Danny Bonaduce), Christopher (Jeremy Gelbwaks/Brian Forster), Tracy (Suzanne Crough), and manager Reuben Kincaid (David Madden). Whether singing lead, making dinner, or solving dating dilemmas, Mrs. Partridge proved that the family that plays together stays together.

9. *Murphy Brown* (1988–1998, CBS)

When Murphy Brown (Candace Bergen) gave birth to her son Avery in the 1991–1992 season finale, she also gave birth to a national controversy. Like many career woman of the 1980s and 1990s, Brown's character hadn't thought about children until an unplanned pregnancy resulted in a decision to raise a child on her own. Attracting criticism from then–Vice President Dan Quayle, and inciting a national "family values" debate, Murphy Brown became a cause célèbre for single mothers everywhere.

10. *Malcolm in the Middle* (2000–, FOX)

Jane Kaczmarek's portrayal of beleaguered Lois is perhaps the most realistic depiction of modern motherhood on television. A master of psychological warfare, she is the first to dole out punishment to her brood of mischievous sons— Malcolm (Frankie Muniz), Reese (Justin Berfield), Dewey (Erik Per Sullivan), and Francis (Christopher Kennedy Masterson). She is also the first to defend them. Just try putting her kids on Ritalin or failing them in school, and this department store clerk mom will attack with the ferocity of a mother wolf protecting her cubs.

Honorable Mentions

1. The Donna Reed Show (1958–1966, ABC)
With starched collars and whiter-than-white aprons, Donna
Stone (Donna Reed) easily addressed the adolescent angst
of Mary (Shelley Fabares) and Jeff (Paul Peterson). Meanwhile, Donna Reed was also playing "mother" behind the
scenes, acting as one of the show's producers and sometime
director.

2. My Mother the Car (1965–1966, NBC)
Perhaps the most unique depiction of a mother on the small
screen, Gladys Crabtree (voiced by Ann Sothern) is reincar-
nated as her son Dave's 1928 Porter convertible.

3. Bewitched (1964–1973, ABC)
Sure, mothers do miraculous things every day, but West-
port, Connecticut, witch Samantha Stevens (Elizabeth Montgomery) could really work some magic. While attempting
to reconcile her powers with her role as suburban housewife, she and husband Darrin (Dick York, Dick Sargent)
had two children, Tabitha and Adam, both of whom inherited mom's witchy ways.

4. Good Times (1974–1979, CBS)
Struggling to raise three children in the South Chicago
projects, Florida Evans, played by Esther Rolle, manages to
keep her kids J.J., Michael, and Thelma on the straight and
narrow despite her husband's death.

5. Kate and Allie (1984–1989, CBS)
Two recently divorced women, Kate (Susan St. James) and
Allie (Jane Curtain), move into a New York brownstone

with their children, creating interesting parenting challenges.

6.   *Absolutely Fabulous* (1992–1995, BBC)

Edina Monsoon (Jennifer Saunders) is idly rich, overindulgent—she smokes, she drinks, she dabbles in drugs and spiritual trends, and has a thing for Christian LaCroix clothing—an incompetent PR agent, and . . . a mother. While not a perfect role model for daughter Saffron (Julia Sawalha), her true colors show through when she saves Saffie from a loveless marriage.

7.   *The X-Files* (1993–2002, FOX)

It's hard enough being a single mom, but being a single mom on the run from nefarious black ops agents while worrying that you've been impregnated by an alien? Agent Dana Scully handles it all with x-emplary aplomb.

Ellen Leventry is a freelance writer living, working, and watching a lot of television in New York City. She has written for publications such as *The Denver Post, Publishers Weekly,* Beliefnet.com, and TheStreet.com.

The Ten Best Books about Motherhood You'll Ever Read

By Jana Riess

It's bad form to begin any essay with an apology. However, I have to admit that I don't know whether these ten selections will indeed be the best motherhood books you'll ever read. But I do know that they are ten books that have spoken to me in a deep and memorable way, and I hope they resonate with your experience, as well. Selecting them has been something of a challenge. The list is, to say the least, impressionistic; what mom in the world has the time or the energy to master the voluminous literature on motherhood?

Instead, I opted for the far less scientific approach of shamelessly soliciting the opinions of all my favorite readers who are moms, including my own mother. So I have had the delightful experience of reading the books they suggested and discussing them together. What has emerged most clearly, at least for me, is how diverse and wonderfully individual the experience of motherhood is. These books reflect a bit of that marvelous particularity, unified only by the extent to which we all desperately love our kids.

I've included several memoirs, a stinging social commentary, two anthologies, one of those ubiquitous advice books, and a sampling of literature. What strikes me as I look at the final list is how geared it is toward *early* motherhood—pregnancy, birth, and the first few crazy years of parenting. Because I'm in these early stages myself, these are the books that have supported me most discernibly. I think that twenty years from now, I will be looking for wise books on having an empty nest or (God willing) becoming a grandmother. For now, these will have to do.

1. *Operating Instructions: A Journal of My Son's First Year* (1993)

My husband read this aloud to me in those first days after coming home from the hospital, when I was nursing our infant daughter. I found the first weeks of breast-feeding to be fairly painful—pain that was only exacerbated as my entire chest heaved from laughing over this book. Anne Lamott is unparalleled in her no-holds-barred frankness, as she describes the trials and triumphs of her first year as a mother. She is also remarkable in her dry wit and lucid cultural commentary.

2. *Expecting Adam: A True Story of Birth, Rebirth,
   and Everyday Magic* (1999)

Martha Beck's moving memoir about expecting a child with Down syndrome is poignant, funny, and full of wisdom. Beck describes her transformation from a success-driven Harvard graduate student to someone who became open to both pain and joy through the experience of having a special needs child. It's a book about losing control and gain-

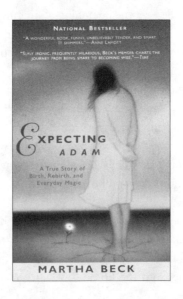

ing perspective, about surrendering cultural status in a quest for compassionate understanding. Beck never succumbs to maudlin sentimentality (a syrupy feature of many other books about children with special needs), but readers may find the tears rolling nonetheless.

3. *Great with Child: Reflections on Faith, Fullness, and Becoming a Mother* (2002)

In the interest of full disclosure, I should acknowledge that this third and final memoir on my top-ten list was penned by my longtime friend Debra Rienstra. Rienstra writes beautifully of her third pregnancy and birth, placing her own experience in the larger social context of advice manuals and changing cultural norms about pregnancy and motherhood. She also plumbs literature for deeply resonant imagery about women's bodies, using a particularly gorgeous Lucille Clifton poem to demonstrate our culture's ambivalence about female beauty.

4. *The Girlfriends' Guides* (an ongoing franchise that began in 1995)

Yes, I have all of the "What to Expect" books on my shelves, and I do consult them periodically. But in the end, those books lack an emotional passion that I need from advice literature. Motherhood is such a zany and *un*expected experience that it doesn't easily lend itself to month-by-month analyses, development charts, and (worst of all) strict dietary regimens. So, when I get down on myself after reading a "What to Expect" chapter, I treat myself with a romp through one of Vicki Iovine's Girlfriends' Guides. The first one hooked me with its hilarious, chatty take on pregnancy, and the second—on the first year of motherhood—cheered me up like no other parenting book could. Iovine has followed these with guides on the toddler years and a just-for-moms manual on "getting your groove back." It's very funny stuff.

5. *The Price of Motherhood: Why the Most Important Job in the World Is Still the Least Valued* (2001)

Wow, and wow again. Ann Crittenden's powerful indictment of the economic costs of motherhood is a call to arms for the American nation. America, she says, pays fluid lip service to the importance of mothers, but then punishes mothers economically if they decide to be full-time caregivers. Our economy is based on the presence of these caregivers, yet assigns no real value to their work. Crittenden spends a chapter analyzing "the invention of the unproductive housewife" and another exposing the "mommy tax." Perhaps most damning is her careful calculation of how much a wife is actually worth. How, she asks, can our culture bring children up without putting women down? This book will make you wince, and—it is hoped—spur you to action.

6. *The Mother Dance: How Children Change Your Life* (1998)

I read this book in about twenty sittings, which is a far cry from my premotherhood habit of reading from cover to cover in just one truffle-endowed evening. Such transformations are the sort of changes that Harriet Lerner might have chronicled in this wise, warm book about the ongoing balancing act that is motherhood. My own favorite chapter is entitled "Enough Guilt for Now, Thank You," but other moms will probably relate most strongly to the final section,

"What Your Mother Never Told You." Lerner draws from her own experience and also shares stories of other women on the front lines of motherhood.

7. *Mothers Who Think: Tales of Real-Life Parenthood* (1999)

This anthology of motherhood essays grew out of Salon. com's evocative Web site of the same name. The essays are, as promised, impressively thoughtful. Susan Straight reflects on the uncertainty of being a single mom to her three daughters in "One Drip at a Time," the title stemming from Straight's inability to fix her leaky faucets. Beth Kephart describes the exhilarating pain of her autistic son's determination to play soccer in "The Line Is White, and It Is Narrow." Kate Moses also provides a couple of beautiful essays, and Elizabeth Rapoport tickles the funny bone with "How Many Fathers Does It Take to Screw in a Lightbulb?"

8. *Mother Reader: Essential Writings on Motherhood* (2001)

More serious and literary than the *Mothers Who Think* anthology, this collection offers short pieces by Margaret Mead, Doris Lessing, Margaret Atwood, Toni Morrison, Alice Walker, and others. Particularly poignant are excerpts from Sylvia Plath's journal, written while she was trying to conceive and on the day of her son's birth; she committed suicide some months later. Other essays don't have quite the despair that characterizes Plath's, but they flirt with darkness, as when Ursula LeGuin reflects on the divergent motherhood choices of various women of letters, including Louisa May Alcott and her most famous character, Jo March. This anthology is certainly not all sweetness and light, but it offers an important counterweight to the many books that suggest that the world's toughest job is a walk in the park.

9. *Demeter and Persephone* (available in many editions, including Edith Hamilton's *Mythology* [1942])

This is certainly my most quixotic choice—it's not contemporary, but nearly three thousand years old, and it's a short myth, not a full-length book. The ancient Greek tale of Demeter, the goddess of Earth, and her daughter, Persephone, is one of the most enduring stories of the bond between mother and child. In a nutshell, Demeter and Persephone's quiet and happy life is destroyed when nasty old Hades, king of the Underworld, seizes Persephone to be his bride. A struggle ensues where the gods take sides (don't they always?) with the eventual result that Persephone lives eight months out of the year with her mother and the other four in Hell. During those four months, the myth holds, Demeter is so bereaved that she causes Earth to undergo a barren and frozen winter season. Winter is a startlingly accurate metaphor for the pain women experience when the sacred mother-child bond is broken.

10. *The Joy Luck Club* (1989)

It's surprising to realize the dearth of quality fiction that deals with issues of motherhood. As increasing numbers of women become published novelists, this is beginning to change, and in future years I have no doubt that we'll see an explosion of excellent novels that address this foundational experience. Amy Tan's novel is pioneering in this respect. By chronicling the lives and loves of three generations of Chinese and Chinese American women, Tan tangibly demonstrates how the courageous actions of the past can change and empower women in the present. She has an amazing capacity to create strong, developed, and plausibly flawed characters, and her novel speaks to the depths of the love and pain that mothers experience.

Jana Riess, the Religion Book Review Editor for *Publishers Weekly,* is the author of *The Spiritual Traveler: Boston and New England.*

❧

From her perch on the crescent of the harvest moon, the Holy Lady looked down and smiled at her imperfect children. The angels attending that night felt little twinges of longing to be in human form, if for only a few minutes. They wanted to rock, they wanted to roll, they wanted to feel the peculiarly human feeling of having a perfect night in an imperfect world. . . . So it is when an umbilical cord of love flows up from the earth and down from the sky.

—Rebecca Wells, *Divine Secrets of the Ya-Ya Sisterhood*

The Ten Best Movies about Motherhood You'll Ever See

By Wendy Schuman

There have been plenty of movies made about mothers— caring moms, scary moms, self-centered moms, saintly moms, pushy moms, and surrogate moms, among others. It was a tough choice, but the following are the movies that made me either laugh or cry or simply feel good about being a mom. There are ten top selections and five honorable mentions; so curl up with a bowl of popcorn and a box of tissues, and enjoy.

1.   *Terms of Endearment*

Perhaps the most insightful mother-daughter film ever made, *Terms of Endearment* beautifully depicts the lifelong push-pull relationship between the generations. Emma (Debra Winger) spends most of her adult life trying to es-

Shirley MacLaine and Debra Winger in *Terms of Endearment*. © Bettmann/Corbis

cape the clutches of her strong-willed, manipulative, and utterly devoted mother, Aurora (Shirley MacLaine). Emma rebels, marries, and moves away with a guy her mother hates (deservedly, as it turns out). But Mom and daughter gradually become reconciled when Emma becomes a mother herself. (Warning: Though mostly hilarious, the film has an almost unbearably sad finale.) This 1983 film won five Oscars, including Best Picture and Best Actress for Shirley MacLaine.

Great Mom Moment: The terminally ill Emma manages to get inside the head of her sullen preteen son and absolve his feelings of guilt.

2. Mask

In this gritty 1985 drama based on a true story, Cher plays Rusty Dennis, the single mother of Rocky (Eric Stoltz), a teenage boy with a disfiguring illness that causes his face to look like a bizarre Halloween mask. Cher's a biker mom whose tough-talking, hard-living facade covers a multitude of motherly virtues. She sees her son as he truly is behind his mask—a young man of keen intelligence and humor. Her fierce love and steely determination help him triumph over pain, prejudice, and loneliness.

Great Mom Moment: Rusty's adamant refusal to let the high school principal shunt her son off to a school for the handicapped.

3. Places in the Heart

Sally Field shines as a young widow, Edna Spalding, who lives in rural Texas during the Depression. When her sheriff husband is suddenly killed, Edna must fight to keep the farm going and raise her two children. She does both with love and ferocious dedication, forming an improvised family with other "outcasts"—a blind boarder (John Malkovich) and a black sharecropper (Danny Glover). Hers is a triumph of character—of a good person bringing out the best in others. The ending is one of the most spiritual and powerful on film. Field won Best Actress for her performance.

Great Mom Moment: Fields, trying to be both mother and father after her husband's death, forces herself to whip her son for an infraction and then declares, "I won't do that ever again."

4. One True Thing

Ellen Gulden (Renee Zellweger) is an ambitious young journalist, a Harvard grad who feels closer to her intellectual professor father (William Hurt) than her housewife mother, Kate (Meryl Streep). When her mother is stricken with cancer, Elly is forced to move home to become the kind of caretaker she vowed never to be. Adapted from the book by Anna Quindlen, this film explores the generation gap between stay-at-home moms and their career-driven daughters. Elly learns much more about the mother who gave everything to her home and family, not sacrificially, but with great creativity and a sense of fun. And she ultimately finds the nurturer within herself.

Great Mom Moment: Kate, on a family drive, pointing out "baby cows" and smiling proudly as her precocious little girl corrects her: "Those are calves, Mom."

5. *Parenthood*

This deeply truthful comedy, directed by Ron Howard, will have you nodding in recognition and laughing uncontrollably at the same time. The film follows three generations of a large family who each wrestle with the question "What's a good parent?" Mom characters include Karen (Mary Steenburgen), who wants a fourth child though her husband (Steve Martin) has lost his job; Susan (Harley Kozak) whose husband (Rick Moranis) is obsessed with raising their four-year-old daughter to be a genius; and Helen (Dianne Wiest), a divorced mother struggling to do her best by her two tough teenagers.

Great Mom Moment: Karen's fierce defense of mothering as an occupation—"This is something I'm good at." Helen's attempt to balance the needs of her kids—agreeing with her dumped daughter that "men are scum" and then trying to salvage the self-esteem of her son, who's overheard the comment.

6. *Lorenzo's Oil*

Based on the true story of Michaela (Susan Sarandon) and Augusto Odone (Nick Nolte), whose young son, Lorenzo (Zack O'Malley Greenburg), is stricken with ALD, an incurable degenerative disease. The Odones turn the medical establishment upside down in their efforts to help their son—even doing their own investigation and convincing reluctant researchers to go after a cure based on ingredients in olive oil (the "Lorenzo's Oil" of the title). Michaela in particular never gives up on Lorenzo, whom she always sees as "gifted" and "extraordinary," even as his body betrays him. In the end, her marternal perseverance is rewarded.

Great Mom Moment: At a support group for parents of children with ALD, Michaela heroically reveals deficiencies in conventional treatment—releasing an outpouring of pent-up frustration from other parents.

7. Little Women

Every little girl who has ever read *Little Women* wants a mother like Marmee, the tower of strength who holds the family together while Papa is off fighting in the Civil War. In the 1994 film version, Susan Sarandon plays Marmee as a proto-feminist, a font of warmth and wisdom who encourages her four individualistic daughters to follow their own dreams.

Great Mom Moment: Though poor, Marmee gives each girl her own little copy of *Pilgrim's Progress* for Christmas, each in a different color. She champions Jo's right to pursue a writing career rather than make an advantageous marriage.

8. Country

Jessica Lange as Jewel Ivy, mother of two and long-suffering Iowa farm wife, stands up to a government bureaucracy that threatens to bankrupt all the farms in the area. Jewel is shown cooking in almost every scene—she's the kind of mom who can whip up mashed potatoes with her baby on one hip, while thinking up strategies to save the family farm. She's a much stronger character than her hunk of a husband Gil (Sam Shepard).

Great Mom Moment: During a tornado, Jewel helps save her teenage son from suffocating under a truckload of grain.

9. *Auntie Mame*

One of the most uplifting, life-affirming Mom movies of the last fifty years isn't even about a mom. This classic comedy, made in 1958, features Rosalind Russell as Mame Dennis, a flamboyant New York sophisticate who takes in her orphaned nephew, Patrick, and brings him up in a glamorous bohemian world in what today would be called an "alternative lifestyle." Her philosophy, with which she inculcates young Patrick: "Life's a banquet, and most poor suckers are starving to death!" (Don't confuse *Auntie Mame* with its far-inferior film musical offspring *Mame,* starring Lucille Ball.)

Great Mom Moment: Mame suggests that Patrick write down all the words he's heard in her household that he doesn't understand. Patrick comes up with a laundry list—from libido to free love to Karl Marx. Mame: "Oh, my my my my, what an eager little mind [takes the list]. You won't need some of these words for months and months."

10. *As Good as It Gets*

In her Oscar-winning role, Helen Hunt plays Carol, a single mom who has the double whammy of having a chronically ill child and being the favorite waitress of an obnoxious guy with obsessive-compulsive disorder (Jack Nicholson). Despite her can-do cheerfulness, Carol becomes a mother lion where her son's well-being is concerned.

Great Mom Moment: Hunt has to explain to a shockingly self-absorbed Nicholson that she can't come back to work to serve him lunch because she needs to take care of her child.

Honorable Mentions

1. **I Remember Mama** (heartwarming 1948 black-and-white classic)
2. **The Joy Luck Club** (Chinese immigrant moms conflict with their Americanized daughters)
3. **Mermaids** (Cher as a quirky mom who embarrasses daughter Winona Ryder)
4. **Mother** (Albert Brooks moves back in with his difficult mother, Debbie Reynolds, to try to understand his problems with women)
5. **Stepmother** (Julia Roberts and Susan Sarandon spar over the latter's children)

Wendy Schuman is the family producer for Beliefnet.com and the family producer at home (of two kids, Corinne and Andrew). She was formerly executive editor of *Parents Magazine* and lives in Monclair, New Jersey.

The Ten Best Songs about Motherhood You'll Ever Hear

By Ellen Leventry

1. "M-O-T-H-E-R"
(Written by Howard Johnson, circa 1915)
" 'M' is for many things she gave me" . . . and the many times this song has been sung to mothers around the world. This lyrical list adeptly describes the many qualities that makes mom so memorable.

2. *"Que Sera Sera"*

(By Ray Evans, as sung by Doris Day, from *Golden Girl: Columbia Recordings 1944–1966,* 1956)

Featured in Alfred Hitchcock's *The Man Who Knew Too Much,* this is the granddaddy, rather, grandmommy of all mother-giving-advice songs. With it's simple refrain of "Whatever will be, will be," "Que Sera Sera" was followed by such philosophical favorites as the Supremes' "You Can't Hurry Love" and Smokey Robinson and the Miracles' "Shop Around."

3. *"Golden Slumbers"* and *"Good Night"*

(By Paul McCartney/Thomas Dekker, sung by Paul McCartney, *Abbey Road,* 1969)

(By John Lennon, sung by Ringo Starr, from *The Beatles,* 1968)

No list of songs about mothers and mothering would be complete without at least one lullaby, and McCartney and Lennon have provided two contemporary classics.

4. *"Lady Madonna"*

(By John Lennon and Paul McCartney, as sung by the Beatles, from *Beatles #1,* 1968)

It's often said that mothers have the patience of saints. Lennon and McCartney take it one step further in this 1968 release, imbuing their exhausted working, single matron with the quiet fortitude of Mother Mary herself.

5. *"Family Hands"*

(By Mary Chapin Carpenter, sung by Mary Chapin Carpenter, from *Hometown Girl,* 1987)

"Raised by the women who are stronger than you know/A patchwork quilt of memory only women could have sewn," sings the daughter to her father on reaching his boyhood home. Offering up a unique perspective, Chapin proves that behind every good man is a great mother and grandmother.

6. *"Mother's Day Song"*
(By Adam Sandler, as performed on *Saturday Night Live,* 1993)
If there's one thing all mothers must have in ample supply, it's a good sense of humor. At times bawdy, at other times bucolic, Adam Sandler's tongue-in-cheek tune is the perfect homage to mom and her funny bone.

7. *"Mama"*
(By the Spice Girls and Stannard & Rowe, sung by the Spice Girls, from *Spice,* 1997)
Leave it to the Spice Girls to remind the world that moms truly have "Girl Power." In this 1997 hit, the girls go from rebellious teens to respectful adult daughters.

8. *"A Song for Mama"*
(By Kenneth "Babyface" Edmonds, as sung by Boyz II Men, from *Evolution,* 1997)
With this soulful and spiritual single, the boys offer up their sincere thanks to the women that have brought them through thick and thin. This top 40 hit was also featured in the movie *Soul Food.*

9. *"Heart of the House"*
(By Alanis Morissette, sung by Alanis Morissette, from *Supposed Former Infatuation Junkie,* 1998)
Ever catch yourself saying something only your mother would say? Sure, we all have. Alanis Morissette puts that

feeling of surprised recognition into words on this cut from her sophomore effort. By exploring the similarities between mother and daughter, she sees her mother in herself.

10. "A New Day Has Come"
(Written by Stephan Moccio and Aldo Nova, sung by Celine Dion, from *A New Day Has Come,* 2002)
Capturing the anguish of a difficult conception ("Everyone told me to be strong/Hold on and don't shed a tear") and the absolute joy of birth ("I can't believe/I've been touched by an angel with love"), Celine Dion draws on her own experience in this inspiring anthem.

Ellen Leventry is a freelance writer living, working, and listening to a lot of music in New York City. She has written for publications such as *The Denver Post, Publishers Weekly,* Beliefnet.com, and TheStreet.com.

Interlude ✒

My mom is one of the bravest people I know. She's not fazed by anything, which gave me an instant fearlessness growing up.

—Charlize Theron

I'm a product of the welfare system, but Mom was an inspiration.

—Sarah Jessica Parker

For a great role model, I had only to look across the breakfast table at my mother. Life tested her, and she didn't break or become bitter; she found the strength to keep going.

—Cindy Crawford

While I prefer not to be like my mother as an actress, I do honestly aspire to be like her in real life. She is absolutely unflappable, with a delightful sense of humor.

—Gwyneth Paltrow

My mother, Bea, was my best friend and the most irrepressible, fun-loving person who ever lived.

—Joan Rivers

My desire to have kids came from my mom Shirley's positive example.

—Annette Benning

FIFTEEN

Every Mom Is Supermom

I remember staring down at William after he was born and seeing a being totally incapable of anything other than selfish demands. He had no language, virtually no strength, no discernable awareness of self, and the barest ability to communicate. He couldn't even hold his head up. All he could do was suck, grasp, startle, and cry—yet that was sufficient. I adored the helpless baby, and I couldn't think of anything better than William. It's amazing that you can love something so small, so

uncomplicated, so demanding—so completely, so uncondition-
ally.

—Leslie Nichols
Mayport, Florida

Whenever I held my newborn babe in my arms, I used to think
what I did and what I said to him would have an influence, not
only on him, but on everyone he meets, not for a day, or a year,
but for all time and for eternity. What a challenge, what a joy!
—Rose Kennedy

Now that I have my own children, I understand in a new way
that if you love something, your children will want to love it

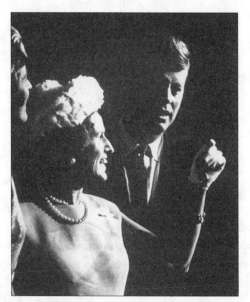

Rose F. Kennedy with son John F. Kennedy at
Democratic Convention in 1960.
© Julian Wasser/Timepix

*too. As parents, we have a chance to help our children go be-
yond us, and to start them off on a lifelong voyage of discovery
and self-discovery.*

—Caroline Kennedy
Schlossberg

Children are likely to live up to what you believe of them.
—Lady Bird Johnson

*When the kids are doing things all together as a group, that's
what makes you think, "Oh, boy, I can do this tomorrow."*
—Bobbi McCaughey

If I can do this, I can do anything.
—Sara Evans

Ten Great Moms of the Twentieth Century

By Therese J. Borchard

They are activists, humorists, Holocaust survivors, writers,
first ladies, and missionaries. But first and foremost, they
are moms. And, in my opinion, some of the best. As a
brand-new mom, I could learn a lesson or two from the vet-
erans. So here is a list of my blue-ribbon picks.

1. Erma Bombeck
She was the funniest mother in America, with an uncanny
ability to bemuse fellow moms with hilarious twists on

cleaning toilets and carpools of whiny kids. For more than thirty years her clippings occupied the most coveted real estate in middle-class homes—the refrigerator—where she'd offer invaluable insight and a dose of comedy amid lost socks, bad report cards, and dirty laundry. In her more than 4,500 columns syndicated in 900 papers nationwide, she confessed her imperfections with a refreshing, self-deprecating humor that became her trademark.

Fueled by the idealized picture of TV mothers such as Harriet Nelson *(Ozzie and Harriet)* and Jane Wyatt *(Father Knows Best),* Erma won the hearts of housewives when she admitted that her kids "were the ones the prime-time mothers forbade their kids to play with," and if she'd raise her hand to wipe the hair from their eyes, "they'd flinch and call their attorneys."

She began writing her column, "At Wit's End," in 1965 at age thirty-seven, when Matthew, the youngest of her three children, started school. Within a year, she gained a huge following as her words were printed in newspapers across America and eventually between the covers of fifteen best-selling books. Diagnosed with polycystic kidney disease at the age of twenty, Erma eventually suffered from kidney failure and died in 1996 of complications from a kidney transplant at the age of sixty-nine.

2. Barbara Bush

From the first minute she entered the public eye during her husband's campaign for political office, she became "everybody's grandmother," exuding a rare warmth and genuineness, keen whit and forthrightness, that won her enormous popularity throughout the country and abroad. Perhaps her relaxed manner and sincere compassion evolved from the

Former First Lady Barbara Bush with daughter Dorothy and
grandchild Ellie LeBlond. © David Valdez/White House/Timepix

hardship of losing her first daughter, Robin, to leukemia
when the little girl was not quite four, a tragedy that the former first lady says will make her husband George and her
"love every living human more."

As the mother of four sons, one daughter, and fourteen
grandchildren, she fulfills her role as America's endearing
grandmother by reading aloud stories to children at schools
or as part of her national radio program called "Mrs. Bush's
Story Time" and by her tireless efforts for children's literacy.

3. *Donna Martin*
Two kids are enough headache and hassle for the average
American family. But not for the Texan-native mom of
nine-year-old daughter LaDonna and fifteen-year-old son
Princeton, who convinced her husband, the pastor of
Bennett Chapel Missionary Baptist Church, to adopt four

neglected and abused kids. She received her inspiration from her own mother, Murtha Cartwright, who gave birth to eighteen children and raised them in the small, predominantly African American community of Possum Trot, near the Texas–Louisiana border.

Despite the extra attention her developmentally disabled son already demanded and her husband's modest income that barely fed the family, Donna drove sixty miles to the town of Lufkin to meet with a social worker to inquire how she could adopt at-risk children. In less than a year, Mercedes and Tyler joined the Martin family; Terri and Joshua came next.

Moreover, Donna and her husband encouraged their church's congregation of fifty families to love and care for one or more of the thousand black children who are up for adoption in the Texas child-welfare system. The result was miraculous. By the summer of 2002, seventy-six children were placed in permanent homes and even more in foster homes.

4. *Martha Beck*

Place yourself in the manically competitive and overachieving environment of Harvard, where girls schedule abortions when unplanned pregnancies threaten their academic and professional progress and a new dad is reprimanded by his professor for skipping a day of class to witness the birth of his first child. While pursuing your doctorate in sociology, you discover you have conceived a baby with Down syndrome. Your friends advise you to terminate the pregnancy. But you carry the baby to full term. And you are changed forever.

You are Martha Beck, and you feel like it when you read her riveting memoir, *Expecting Adam,* about the little boy with Down syndrome who brought more love, joy, and magic into her life than any Ivy League achievement could ever hope to. On every page of her autobiographical tale, she describes her painful and poignant transformation, in which she unlearns everything she was taught by the sharpest and shrewdest of minds in order to recognize and cherish true beauty and wisdom. And in doing so, she is an inspiration to all mothers caring for children with disabilities.

5. Mother Teresa

She may not be a mother in the traditional sense, but she fed more mouths in one day than most moms do in a lifetime. Born as Agnes Gonxha Bojaxhiu in Skopje, Yugoslavia, she joined the Sisters of Loreto at age eighteen and moved to Calcutta, India, where she took her final vows and taught at St. Mary's High School for twenty years.

Mother Teresa. © Catholic News Service

Every day of those two decades she saw the poverty and suffering of the people outside the convent wall. In 1946 she obtained permission from her superiors to devote herself exclusively to working among the poorest of the poor in the slums of Calcutta. She started with a school for homeless children and later opened clinics, orphanages, homes for the dying, leper colonies, and food centers. In 1950 she founded her own order, the Missionaries of Charity, which today comprises more than a thousand sisters and brothers and has spread to other countries in its many relief projects. The modern saint died in 1997, but her mission "to care for the hungry, the naked, the homeless, the crippled, the blind, the lepers, all those people who feel unwanted, unloved, uncared for throughout society" lives on in the humble sisters who wear the plain white sari with a blue border and in all those who have been inspired by her message to love well.

6. *Bobbi McCaughey*

At age twenty-nine, Bobbi McCaughey gave birth to America's first set of living septuplets, shocking medical experts and the general public. Add Bobbi's first daughter, Mikayla, and that makes eight kids to dress in the morning, feed every three or four hours, potty train, and bathe before bed.

Within a few hours of Bobbi's cesarean section on November 19, 1997, the small-town couple of Carlisle, Iowa, became instant celebrities, showered with lifetime supplies of diapers and baby food. But just because she's famous and moved into a large home donated to the family doesn't mean Bobbi's days aren't jampacked with a mother's share of challenges times eight. Born prematurely, all seven were on respirators as infants and two children suffer from cerebral palsy. With all outings impossible—even a trip to the local supermarket—you'd think this homebound mom would go stir crazy. But the devout Baptist doesn't let herself get frazzled. Her secret? "You just have to trust that God's going to take care of you," she says, a bit of insight from a pro.

7. *Raja Indurski-Weksler*

In June of 1941, German soldiers invaded Vilna, Lithuania, and forced Raja Indurski-Weskler and her family to evacuate their home. After hiding her family in a series of "actions" (where Jews—packed in the Vilna Ghetto—were executed to fulfill a quota set by the German police), Raja became an unlikely hero, repeatedly risking her own life to ensure the survival of her daughter.

The astute and determined mother first sewed jewelry and coins into the linings of her coat, using such treasures to barter her way to the "right," where the soldiers directed the stronger women capable of working, and thus had a greater chance to live. At one point, she emptied her backpack of all possessions and hauled her eleven-year-old daughter on her back, shoving her way through a crowd of desperate women fighting for their lives while soldiers kicked and beat them to determine who was resilient.

Once at the concentration camp, Raja disguised her daughter as a teenager, smuggling a stuffed bra and headscarves from the clothing depot where she worked so that the short, frail girl would appear taller and shapelier. That way the two would not be separated and Raja could literally force her daughter to survive, which she did—and lives to tell about in her powerful account appropriately entitled *Thanks to My Mother*.

Marian Wright Edelman.
© Children's Defense Fund

8. *Marian Wright Edelman*

She was only twenty-four years old when she became the first African American woman admitted to the Mississippi Bar, directing the NAACP Legal Defense and Educational Fund office in Jackson, Mississippi. A few years later she moved to the nation's capital to join forces with Martin Luther King Jr. as counsel for the Poor People's March. There she founded the Washington Research Project, the parent body of the Children's Defense Fund, whose mission is to ensure every child has a fair and healthy start in life.

As president of the CDF, Marian has spent thirty plus years fighting for better healthcare, education, and economic support for disadvantaged and at-risk kids, earning her a reputation as one of the nation's leading advocates for children. She is the recipient of a host of honorary degrees and awards, such as the prestigious Presidential Medal of Freedom, and she is the proud mother of three sons: Joshua, Jonah, and Ezra.

9. *Jacqueline Onassis*

She was the epitome of grace and dignity, forever remembered wearing her round sunglasses and headscarf or three-strand pearl necklace as an icon of style. But her good taste extended beyond her elegant wardrobe and her affinity for the classic arts. She demanded privacy, especially when it came to her family, taming an aggressive media to respect her distance, so that she could devote herself entirely to her children.

Always and everywhere, her kids came first. "If you bungle raising your children, nothing much else matters in life," she once said. So while most people sought the limelight, she avoided it, and focused her attention on John Jr. and Caroline.

The reluctant celebrity became a notorious picture of composure and poise the country depended on in the days and years following the 1963 assassination of her husband. And in mothering a daughter and son with such unabashed loyalty and bravery amid a personal and public tragedy, she became a mother to a nation, until her death in 1994.

10. *Nancy Johnson Guenin (my mother)*

I'm lucky. I have the best role model of a mother in my own mom, who raised four daughters born within three years of each other with little help from her husband. As a mother who can hardly handle one boy, I now look to my mom in awe and wonder how on earth she managed a set of newborn twins with a one- and two-year-old at her knees.

But she loved it, and still does. She looked on motherhood as the noblest profession, the highest honor to be be-

Nancy holds grandson David.

stowed on a woman. Her four girls were and are her world, which is how she succeeded at making us feel as if we were God's most special creatures, filling the home with happy memories despite my father's leaving her.

Now the mother of all girls does the same for her four grandsons, loving them into strong boys and men, empowering them with confidence, and instilling them in them the values and morals that will make their world a better place.

Honorable Mention:

Nancy Borchard *(my mother-in-law)*
This list would be incomplete without including the woman who welcomed me into her family as another daughter the moment she got wind that her son "was serious about this one." I had no test to pass or time to wait.

Her love was instant, her attitude evident in the framed saying she gave me on our first Christmas together as a new family. It read, "Daughter In Law: God gave us a special one when he sent an angel to marry our son." There are no pretensions, no squabbles or strains that exist between many daughters and mothers-in-law. Just a beautiful friendship, which I value more and more every day.

Interlude ❧

The most important person on earth is a mother. She cannot claim the honor of having built Notre Dame Cathedral. She has built something more magnificent than any cathedral—a dwelling for an immortal soul, the tiny perfection of her baby's body. The angels have not been blessed with such a grace. They cannot share in God's creative miracle to bring new saints to Heaven. Only a human mother can. Mothers are closer to God the Creator in performing this act of creation. . . . what on God's good earth is more glorious than this: to be a mother?

—Joseph Cardinal Mindszenty

Mother is the name for God in the lips and hearts of children.

—William Makepeace
Thackeray

When God thought of mother, He must have laughed with satisfaction . . . so rich, so deep, so divine, so full of soul, power, and beauty, was the conception.

—Henry Ward Beecher

Stretch Marks on My Heart

By Therese J. Borchard

I never liked baby-sitting when I was younger. In fact, I'd rather wash dishes or pull weeds than to comfort a crying baby. They scared me, especially the newborns. I thought they'd break if you held them the wrong way. So when I found out I was pregnant, one thought—actually two— wouldn't leave me the three trimesters of bloatedhood:

What if I didn't like being a mom? And what if I wasn't good at it?

It's not like you can return the kid for a refund. The majority of us feel compelled to nurture and raise the tiny thing that has emerged from us even if they have taken our bodies hostage for nine months (and a half) and wreaked all kinds of havoc, from severe heartburn to an overactive bladder.

My anxiety worsened every time someone would tell me, well intentioned, "Your life will never be the same." "Savor your free time while you got it." "Enjoy your last full night's sleep."

Until July 5, 2001, my work—writing and compiling books—was what energized me. That is to say, in addition to my marriage and friendships. I began to resent the tiny bean inside for stealing away my dream of becoming someone important: a best-selling author, a famous writer, or something like that.

And I was nervous because I am basically a selfish person. Would I have to play with this little tyke or would he be good and let me get some work done during the day? As my due date came (and then went), a depression set in. I knew there was no going back. What the ladies said were true—my life would never be the same.

Yep. The fireworks on the evening of the Fourth of July awoke the little guy inside me like an alarming clock signaling he had overslept and was about to miss the grand finale. Good thing he decided to come out on his own, because two more days inside the womb and he would have received his eviction notice.

I guess it is appropriate that the most painful, scariest, but most sacred experience of my life began with an impressive display of explosives that almost blew my friend's arm off at our annual amateur fireworks show. Equally fitting was the fact that David Nels decided to crawl out—or, more accurately, be yanked out of my uterus in an emergency cesarean—on his father's birthday.

From the first minute I laid eyes on my son, as I was stretched out and restrained on the operating table, my concern of whether I would like being a mom vanished immediately. There, before me, was the most beautiful thing I had ever seen in my life. The love that shot through my heart was more penetrating than the needle through my spine just hours before.

My husband could not speak through his tears. He just held little David high enough for me to see his strawberry highlights and deep blue eyes. All I could do was thank God for the miracle in front of me, for giving us the gift of creation.

I love being a mom for all the same reasons other moms do. For all the firsts that we've already had—his first bath, the first time he laughed out loud, his first tears, his first Halloween, the first time he rolled over—and for all the firsts to come: his first day of school, his first T-ball game. I love being a mom for selfish reasons: for the way he makes me feel when I'm nursing him and he looks up at me with that glazed-over expression—the milk buzz—like I just delivered him filet mignon and potatoes au gratin in bed. Or the way his eyes light up when I reach into his crib to pick him up, like I am the only star in his universe. And that sweet, pure smile—the one where I can see my husband's impish dimples—that is the perfect picture of goodness and virtue.

I love being a mom for what philosopher Teilhard de

Chardin called "the chosen part of things"—the stories, memories, and scrapbook events that are found on every page of this book. For the breath of innocence two-month-old David gave me the morning of September 11 when he lay peacefully on my lap, unable to sit up and see the ominous images of horror displayed on our 32-inch television as the two World Trade Towers crumbled to dust, but instead giggled and cooed, filling the room with a sound of hope that echoed through my soul. And for the comic relief he offered the church of grieving families that Friday when he passed (loud) gas during a moment of silence.

The second question that plagued me during my pregnancy—if I would be any good at motherhood—wasn't answered as automatically as the first. But every morning David wakes up breathing (and that time is finally becom-

David's first trip to the beach with Mom.

ing more manageable for a sleepy mom), I grow more confident in my abilities as a caretaker. I have learned how to squeeze in a little me-time, work, and brain exercises so that my mind doesn't go flabby with my belly. I am trying as best as a new mom can to balance my sense of self with the selfless responsibilities of a mother.

And speaking of my belly, I am resigned to the fact—after fifty sit-ups every day for the last three months—that there will be no getting back my once-tight stomach. Unfortunately my zebra stretch marks are here to stay. You won't catch me dead in a halter top or short T (not that I wore them before). But I don't care anymore. Because I proudly wear my war wounds. I earned my Purple Heart in the most honorable of all battles.

I can't argue with those who told me my life would completely change with eight pounds of love. My stretch marks are proof of that. And if you think the ones on my stomach are bad, you should see my heart.

ACKNOWLEDGMENTS

I am grateful to the many contributors whose original stories illumine this book and to the publishers who gave me
permission to reprint sparkling excerpts from their books,
magazines, and newspapers.

A special thanks goes to Melissa Mathews, art teacher,
and the talented children at Eastport Elementary School
(Briayna Cuffie, Andrew Curlings, Caroline Eberhardt, Can-
dace Greene, Takeia Jackson, Tayler Jenson, Moniquequa
Johnson, Josh Kohut, Olivia Reed, Tiffany Stocks, Jennifer
Turner, Alex Wilkinson, Brittany Wilson), and to Victoria
Sames and Kate Stengel, for contributing their beautiful
crayon drawings that are sprinkled throughout these pages.

I am grateful to Kate Potter, who watched my little
David a few days a week, allowing me some uninterrupted
work time. Without her loving care and devotion, I would
still have an unfinished manuscript.

Thank you to my agent, Joe Durepos, and to all the
wonderful professionals at Doubleday, especially Liz Walter,
who so generously connected me to all the happy moms in
her network of writers, family, and friends, and for her invaluable insight along the way, and to Michelle Rapkin,
who shared my enthusiam for the book and shepherded it
through the editorial and production process.

A humongous hug to Mike Leach, coeditor of *I Like*

Being® Catholic and *I Like Being® Married,* who inspired this whole series and who acted as my silent but very involved partner on this book.

And thank you to Eric, my husband; David, my son; and newborn baby Katherine Rose, who make me love being a mom more and more each day.

About the Editor

Therese J. Borchard is a nationally syndicated columnist and coeditor, with Michael Leach, of the bestselling *I Like Being® Catholic: Treasured Traditions, Rituals, and Stories* (Doubleday, 2000), and *I Like Being® Married* (Doubleday, 2002). She holds an M.A. degree in theology from the University of Notre Dame and has published articles in the *Washington Post, Newsday,* the *Detroit Free Press,* the *Baltimore Sun,* the *Houston Chronicle,* the *Dallas Morning News, Publishers Weekly, American Baby,* and Beliefnet.com.

As a regular guest on national television and radio programs, and as a presenter of workshops and seminars around the country, Therese is a leading voice among young people discussing topics such as relationships, marriage, and parenthood. She lives with her husband, Eric, and son, David, in Annapolis, Maryland, where she has just welcomed their second child, Katherine Rose.